HARRAP'S

English Grammar

Compiled by
Gert Ronberg
with
LEXUS

HARRAP
London

First published in Great Britain 1989
by HARRAP BOOKS Ltd
Chelsea House, 26 Market Square,
Bromley, Kent BR1 1NA

© *Harrap Books Ltd* 1989

ISBN 0 245-54746-0

Reprinted 1990 (twice)

Printed and bound in Singapore by
Intellectual Publishing Co.

INTRODUCTION

This grammar of English has been written primarily to meet
the needs of those who are studying English. (And what better
way for the native speaker of English to seek clarification of
problematic areas of English than to see how these have been
presented for the non-native speaker.) Essential rules have
been explained in terms that are as accessible as possible to all
users. Where technical terms have been used then full
explanations have also been supplied. There is also a full
glossary of grammatical terminology on pages 8-16. While
literary aspects of the language have not been ignored, the
emphasis has been placed squarely on modern spoken
English. And contrasts and comparisons have been drawn
between British and American English. This grammar, with
its wealth of lively and typical illustrations of usage, is the ideal
study or reference tool for all levels — from the beginner who
is starting to come to grips with the English language through
to the advanced user who requires a comprehensive and
readily accessible work of reference.

CONTENTS

1.	GLOSSARY OF GRAMMATICAL TERMS	8
2.	ARTICLES	17
	A. Forms	17
	B. Position	18
	C. Use of the Articles	19
	1. Indefinite	19
	2. Definite	21
3.	NOUNS	29
	A. Types	29
	1. Concrete and abstract	29
	2. Common and proper	30
	3. Countable and uncountable	30
	B. Forms	40
	C. Use: Plural versus Singular	48
	D. Genitive	50
	E. Feminines	54
4.	ADJECTIVES	56
	A. Types	56
	B. Forms	56
	C. Use	58
	1. Attributive and predicative	58
	2. Comparison	62
	3. Position	64

		4. Adjectives used as nouns	66
5.	**ADVERBS AND ADVERBIALS**		71
	A.	Types	71
		1. Adverbs	71
		2. Adverbial phrases and clauses	72
	B.	Forms	74
	C.	Use	77
		1. Adverbial functions	77
		2. Adverbs with adjectival forms	78
		3. Position of the adverb	92
6.	**PRONOUNS**		100
	A.	Types	100
	B.	Forms	100
	C.	Use	101
		1. Personal	101
		2. Reflexive	109
		3. Possessive	111
		4. Demonstrative	112
		5. Interrogative	113
		6. Relative	115
		7. Indefinite	120
7.	**VERBS**		133
	A.	Types	133
		1. Regular	133
		2. Irregular	133

	3. Auxiliary	135
B.	Forms	136
	1. Infinitive	136
	2. Present participle	136
	3. Past participle	136
	4. Gerund	136
	5. Present tense	137
	6. Past tense	137
	7. Tense and aspect	138
	8. Mood	138
	9. Voice	139
C.	Use	140
	1. Infinitive	140
	2. Gerund	145
	3. Possessive and the gerund	146
	4. Gerund and the infinitive compared	147
	5. Present participle	151
	6. Present participle and gerund compared	153
	7. Past participle	154
	8. Questions	156
	9. Negations	158
	10. Expressing present time	161
	11. Expressing past time	163
	12. Expressing future time	165

13. Expressing condition 170

14. Subjunctive 173

15. Attitudinal past tense 176

16. Passive 177

17. *Be*, *have*, *do* 180

18. Modal auxiliaries 186

19. *Dare*, *need* 196

20. Prepositional verbs and phrasal verbs 197

21. Tense in indirect speech 202

22. List of irregular verbs 205

23. Auxiliaries *be*, *have* and *do*: forms 212

8. PREPOSITIONS 214

9. CONJUNCTIONS 228

   1. Coordinating 228

   2. Subordinating 231

10. NUMERALS 235

11. SENTENCE STRUCTURE 241

12. NOTES ON SPELLING 247

   INDEX 251

1. GLOSSARY OF GRAMMATICAL TERMS

ABSTRACT NOUN
An abstract noun is one which refers not to a concrete physical object or a person but to a quality or a concept. Examples of abstract nouns are *happiness*, *life*, *length*.

ACTIVE
The active form of a verb is the basic form as in *I remember her*. It is normally opposed to the passive form of the verb as in *she will be remembered*.

ADJECTIVAL NOUN
An adjectival noun is an adjective used as a noun. For example, the adjective *young* is used as a noun in *the young at heart*.

ADJECTIVE
A describing word telling us what something or someone is like (eg *a **small** house*, *the **Royal** Family*, *an **interesting** pastime*).

ADVERB
Adverbs are normally used with a verb to add extra information by indicating **how** the action is done (adverbs of manner), **when**, **where** and **with how much intensity** the action is done (adverbs of time, place and intensity), or **to what extent** the action is done

(adverbs of quantity). Adverbs may also be used with an adjective or another adverb (eg *a **very** attractive girl*, ***very** well*).

APPOSITION A word or a phrase is said to be in apposition to another when it is placed directly after it without any joining word (eg *Mr Jones, **our bank manager**, rang today*).

ARTICLE See DEFINITE ARTICLE and INDEFINITE ARTICLE.

AUXILIARY Auxiliary verbs are used to form verb phrases together with main verbs, eg ***have*** in *I **have** seen* or ***will*** in *she **will** go*. See MODAL .

BASE See INFINITIVE.

BOUND Pronouns are said to be 'bound' when they are used with an accompanying noun. For example, *her* in *her address* is not possible without a word like *address*. Similarly *that* is a bound demonstrative pronoun in *that phone number*. Bound possessive pronouns are also known as possessive adjectives; bound demonstrative pronouns are also known as demonstrative adjectives.

CARDINAL Cardinal numbers are numbers such as *one*, *two*, *ten*, *fourteen*, as opposed to **ordinal** numbers (eg *first*, *second*).

CLAUSE A clause is a group of words which contains at least a subject and a verb: *he said* is a clause. A clause often contains more than this basic information, eg *he said this to her yesterday*. Sentences can be made up of several clauses, eg *he said / he'd call me / if he were free*. See SENTENCE.

COLLECTIVE

A collective noun is one which names a group of people or things but which is singular in form. Examples of collective nouns are *flock* or *fleet*.

COLLOQUIAL

Colloquial language is the sort of language that can be used in everyday informal conversation but is avoided in formal writing such as legal contracts etc.

COMPARATIVE

The comparative forms of adjectives and adverbs are used to compare two things, persons or actions. In English, *more ... than*, *-er than*, *less ... than* and *as ... as* are used for comparison.

COMPOUND

Compound tenses are verb tenses consisting of more than one element. The compound tenses of a verb are formed by the **auxiliary** verbs and the **present** or **past participle**: *I was waiting, they have left*.

Compound nouns are nouns made up of two or more separate words, for example *goalkeeper* or *dinner party*.

CONDITIONAL

This mood is used to describe what someone would do, or something that would happen if a condition were fulfilled (eg *I would come* if I was well; *the chair would have broken* if he had sat on it). It also indicates future in the past, eg *he said he would come*.

CONJUGATION The conjugation of a verb is the set of different forms taken in the particular tenses and moods of that verb.

CONJUNCTION Conjunctions are linking words (eg *and*, *or*, *but*). They may be coordinating or subordinating. Coordinating conjunctions are words like *and*, *or*, *but*; subordinating conjunctions are words like *that*, *whether*, *how*.

CONTINUOUS The continuous form of a verb is formed with *to be* + **present participle**, for example, *I am speaking, he has been speaking, they will be expecting us*. This is also called the 'progressive'.

COUNTABLE A noun is countable if it can form a plural and if it can be used with the indefinite article. Examples of countable nouns are *house, car, dog, sweater*.

DEFINITE ARTICLE The definite article is *the*.

DEMONSTRATIVE Demonstratives are words like *this*, *that*, *these*, *those* which can be either **bound** as in *this book*, *these ideas* or **free** as in *I prefer those*, *I don't want that*.

DIRECT OBJECT A noun or a pronoun which follows a verb without any linking preposition, eg *I met **a friend***. Note that in English a preposition is often omitted, eg *I sent him a present* − *him* is equivalent to *to him* − *a present* is the direct object.

EXCLAMATION	Words or phrases used to express surprise, annoyance etc (eg *what!*, *wow!*; *how lucky!*, *what a nice day!*).
FREE	Pronouns are said to be 'free' when they are used without a noun immediately following. For example, *his* in *this is his* is a free possessive pronoun. Contrast this with *his* as used in *his address*. *Hers* can only be a free possessive pronoun, *her* can only be a bound possessive pronoun. *This* is a free demonstrative pronoun in *what's this?* But it is used as a bound demonstrative pronoun in *this address is his*.
GERUND	A gerund is also called a 'verbal noun'. It has the same form as the **present participle** of a verb, ie base + **-ing**. Examples are: *skiing is fun, I'm fed up with waiting*.
IDIOMATIC	Idiomatic expressions (or idioms), are expressions which cannot normally be understood literally. For example, *he thinks he's the cat's whiskers*.
IMPERATIVE	A mood used for giving orders (eg *stop!*, *don't go!*) or for making suggestions (eg *let's go*).
INDEFINITE PRONOUN	Indefinite pronouns are words that do not refer to a definite person or thing (eg *each*, *someone*).
INDEFINITE ARTICLE	The indefinite article is *a* or *an*.

INDICATIVE

The form of a verb normally used in making statements or asking questions, as in *I like*, *he came*, *we are trying*. It is opposed to the subjunctive, conditional and imperative.

INDIRECT OBJECT

A noun or pronoun standing for somebody or something affected by the action described by the verb and direct object. In *The man wrote his friend a letter*, *his friend* is the indirect object, the direct being *a letter*.

INFINITIVE

The infinitive is the form of the verb as found in dictionaries. Thus *(to) eat*, *(to) finish*, *(to) take* are infinitives.

INTERROGATIVE

Interrogative words are used to ask a **question**. This may be a direct question (**when** *will you arrive?*) or an indirect question (*I don't know* **when** *he'll arrive*). See QUESTION.

MODAL

The modal auxiliaries are the words *can/could*, *may/might*, *must/had to*, *shall/should*, *will/would*. Also *ought to*, *used to*, *dare* and *need*. One of their main features is that question and negative forms are constructed without the use of the auxiliary *do*.

MOOD

The name given to the three main areas within which a verb is conjugated. See INDICATIVE, SUBJUNCTIVE, IMPERATIVE.

NOUN

A word which refers to living creatures, things, places or abstract ideas, eg *postman*, *cat*, *shop*, *passport*, *life*.

NUMBER

The number of a noun indicates whether the noun is **singular** or **plural**.

A singular noun refers to one single thing or person (eg *boy*, *train*) and a plural noun to several (eg *boys*, *trains*).

OBJECT

See DIRECT OBJECT, INDIRECT OBJECT.

OBJECT COMPLEMENT

A noun or adjective immediately following a direct object and describing it. In *they made him chairman* and *they made him happy*, *chairman* and *happy* are the object complements.

ORDINAL

Ordinal numbers are *first*, *second* etc.

PASSIVE

A verb is used in the passive when the subject of the verb does not perform the action but is subjected to it. The passive can be formed with a part of the verb *to be* and the past participle of the verb, eg *he was rewarded*.

PAST PARTICIPLE

The past participle of a verb is the form which is used after *to have*, eg *I have **eaten**, I have **said**, you have **tried***. It is also used to form the passive.

PERSON

In any tense, there are three persons in the singular (1st: *I* ..., 2nd: *you* ..., 3rd: *he/she* ...), and in the plural (1st: *we* ..., 2nd: *you* ..., 3rd: *they* ...).

PHRASAL AND PREPOSITIONAL VERBS

Phrasal and prepositional verbs are verbs of the type *run down* (phrasal) and *look after* (prepositional). They usually have a meaning which is more than the sum of their parts. For example, *he ran down his friends* (as opposed to *he ran down the road*) and *he looked after the cat* (as opposed to *he ran after the cat*).

PLURAL	See NUMBER.
POSSESSIVE	Possessives are used to indicate possession or ownership. They are words like *my/mine*, *your/yours*, *our/ours*.
PREPOSITION	Prepositions are words such as *with*, *in*, *to*, *at*. They are normally followed by a noun or a pronoun.
PRESENT PARTICIPLE	The present participle is the verb form which ends in **-ing**.
PROGRESSIVE	See CONTINUOUS.
PRONOUN	A word which stands for a noun. The main categories of pronouns are:

★ **Personal pronouns** (eg *you*, *him*, *us*)
★ **Possessive pronouns** (eg *mine*, *yours*, *his*)
★ **Reflexive pronouns** (eg *myself*, *himself*)
★ **Interrogative pronouns** (eg *who?*, *what?*, *which?*)
★ **Relative pronouns** (eg *who*, *which*, *that*)
★ **Demonstrative pronouns** (eg *this*, *that*, *these*)
★ **Indefinite pronouns** (eg *something*, *none*)

QUESTION	There are two question forms: **direct** questions stand on their own and require a question mark at the end (eg *when will he come?*); **indirect** questions are introduced by a clause and require no question mark (eg *I wonder when he will come*).

REFLEXIVE	Reflexive verbs 'reflect' the action back onto the subject (eg *I dressed myself*).
SENTENCE	A sentence is a group of words made up of one or more clauses (see CLAUSE). The end of a sentence is indicated by a punctuation mark (usually a full stop, a question mark or an exclamation mark).
SINGULAR	See NUMBER.
SUBJECT	The subject of a verb is the noun or pronoun which performs the action. In the sentences *the train left early* and *she bought a record*, *the train* and *she* are the subjects.
SUBJUNCTIVE	A verb form to indicate wish, supposition and the like which does not take -s in the third person present: *God save the Queen*.
SUPERLATIVE	The form of an adjective or an adverb which is marked by *the most* ..., *the/-est* or *the least* ....
TENSE	Verbs are used in tenses, which indicate when an action takes place, eg in the present, the past, the future.
UNCOUNTABLE	Uncountable nouns are nouns which do not normally take a plural, for example *butter*, *willingness*.
VERB	A 'doing' word, which usually describes an action (eg *to sing*, *to work*, *to watch*). Some verbs describe a state (eg *to be*, *to have*, *to hope*).
VOICE	The two voices of a verb are its active and passive forms.

2. ARTICLES

A. FORMS

a) The indefinite article is **a** before consonants and **an** before vowels:

    a cat   **an owl**

    a dog   **an umbrella**

It is important to bear in mind that the use of **a/an** depends on whether the initial letter of the following word is *pronounced* as a vowel or not. So for example a silent 'h' is preceded by **an**:

    an hour

    an honour

    an heir

The letters 'u' and 'eu' when pronounced as in 'you' are preceded by **a**:

    a university   **a union**

    a eucalpytus tree

With the noun **hotel** either **a** or **an** can be used, although everyday spoken English prefers **a**.

b) The definite article is **the**:

    the cat

    the owl

For emphatic usage this can also be pronounced to rhyme with 'we' as in:

    he's definitely *the* man for the job

The is also pronounced in this way when preceding a word that starts with a vowel as in the above example **the owl**.

B.   POSITION

Articles precede the noun and any adjectives (with or without qualifying adverbs) before the noun:

> **a hat/the hat**
> **a smart hat/the smart hat**
> **a very smart hat/the very smart hat**

However, the words **all** and **both** precede the definite article:

> **they had all the fun**
> **both the men (= both men) were guilty**

And the adverbs **quite** and **rather** normally precede the articles:

> **it was quite/rather a good play**
> **it was quite the best play I've seen**

However, **quite** and **rather** are sometimes found **after** the indefinite article as in:

> **that was a rather unfortunate remark to make**
> **that would be a quite useless task**

The words **too**, **so** and **as** precede the indefinite article together with the adjective:

> **if that is not too great a favour to ask**
> **never have I seen so boring a film**
> **I have never seen as fine an actor as Olivier**

The indefinite article also follows **many**, **such** and **what**:

> **many a man would do the same**
> **she's such a fool**
> **what a performance!**

Note that with **such** an adjective follows the indefinite article, whereas with **so** it precedes it (see also above):

> **I have never seen such a beautiful painting**
> **I have never seen so beautiful a painting**

Mention should also be made of the word **half**, which normally precedes the article:

> **half the world knows about this**
>
> **I'll be back in half a minute**

But if **half** and the noun are taken as a compound, the article comes first, as in:

> **why don't you buy just a half bottle of rum?**

ie a small bottle of rum. But we would normally say:

> **he drank half a bottle of rum**

emphasizing the amount of rum more than the container (the amount might be half the contents of a whole bottle).

C.   USE OF THE ARTICLES

1   THE INDEFINITE ARTICLE (a, an)

Normally the indefinite article is confined to countable nouns, but countability is itself quite a problem in English. See the discussion on p 32.

a)   The generic use, referring to a class

This can be seen in examples like:

> **a mouse is smaller than a rat**

where **a mouse** and **a rat** represent the class of mice or the class of rats. With a slight difference in meaning the definite article can also be used generically. See below, p 22.

Note that generic **man** representing mankind (as opposed to meaning 'a male human being') does not take the article:

> **a dog is man's best friend**

b) With nouns functioning as subject complement or in apposition or following the word **as**:

> **he is a hairdresser**
>
> **she has become a Member of Parliament**
>
> **Miss Behrens, a singer of formidable range, had no problems with the role**
>
> **John Adams, a real tough guy, was leaning casually on the bar**
>
> **he used to work as a skipper**

When the indefinite article is used in such cases, there is a reference to a member of a class. If class membership is irrelevant the article is omitted, as in the following examples, where only one individual is possible:

> **she is now Duchess of York**
>
> **Professor Draper, head of the English department**

If the noun refers to characteristics rather than to membership of a class the article is also omitted (and is always omitted after **turn**):

> **he turned traitor**
>
> **surely you're man enough to stand up to her**

but:

> **be a man!**

If a number of words are listed in apposition then the article can be omitted:

> **Maria Callas, opera singer, socialite and companion of Onassis, died in her Paris flat yesterday**

The definite article **the** is used if the person referred to is well-known (or is being distinguished from another person of the same name):

> **Maria Callas, the opera singer . . .**

c)   *As a preposition*

The indefinite article can be used with the sense 'per', as in:

> **an apple a day keeps the doctor away**
>
> **haddock is £1.80 a pound**
>
> **take two tablets twice a day**

d)   *With little and few*

The indefinite article with these two words indicates something positive (on their own **little** and **few** have a negative meaning):

> **she needs a little attention** (= some attention)
>
> **she needs little attention** (= hardly any attention)
>
> **they have a few paintings** (= some)
>
> **they have few paintings** (= hardly any)

However, **only a little/few** means more or less the same as **little/few** which are less common:

> **I have only a little coffee left** (= hardly any)
>
> **I can afford only a few books** (= hardly any)

Note also the expression **a good few** which means 'quite a lot':

> **there are a good few miles to go yet**
>
> **he's had a good few (to drink)**

2   THE DEFINITE ARTICLE (the)

a)   The definite article is used with both countable and uncountable nouns:

> **the butter** (uncountable)
>
> **the cup** (countable singular)
>
> **the cups** (countable plural)

b) Its most frequent use is with nouns that have already been identified. Thus nobody would say **the man came up to me** unless **the man** had been mentioned earlier in the conversation. **The man** is thus a definite man in the speaker's and listener's mind. However, the noun need not have been mentioned just previously; it is enough that what it refers to has been identified at some stage:

> **switch off the television!**
>
> **don't look into the sun**

c) Like the indefinite article the definite article may be used generically. The slight difference is that the definite article version can sound more scientific:

> **the mouse is smaller than the rat** (compare 1a) above)
>
> **when was the potato first introduced to Europe?**

d) A prepositional phrase after the noun can either define or describe. If it defines, the definite article must be used:

> **I want to wear the trousers on that hanger**
>
> **she has just met the man of her dreams**
>
> **the parcels from Aunt Mary haven't arrived yet**

However, if the prepositional phrase describes or categorizes rather than defines, the article is normally omitted:

> **everywhere we looked we saw trousers on hangers**
>
> **knowledge of Latin and Greek is desirable**
>
> **presence of mind is what he needs**
>
> **I always love receiving parcels from Aunt Mary**

So if I say:

> **the presence of mind that she showed was extraordinary**

the use of **the** is not due to the following **of**-phrase (which only categorizes), but to the fact that a specific instance of presence of mind is referred to, as is shown by the defining relative clause that follows.

However, sometimes **of**-phrases are, as it were, half descriptive and half defining, ie the preceding noun is neither completely general nor completely specific. In such cases the definite article is used:

the women of Paris (= women from Paris, in general)

the children of such families (= children from such families)

e) A large number of nouns omit the article if they refer to **function** or **characteristics** in general rather than the object itself. Such nouns include:

i) institutions, for instance:

church	prison
college	school
court	university
hospital	

Examples:

do you go to church?

she's in hospital again and he's in prison

aren't you going to school today?

Joan is at university

However, American English prefers the definite article with **hospital**:

Wayne is back in the hospital

If the noun refers to the physical object (the building) rather than its function, **the** is used:

walk up to the church and turn right

the taxi stopped at the school

The is also used if a noun is used in a defining sense (see above 2d)):

at the university where his father studied

she's at the university (= the local university)

ii) means of transport preceded by **by**:

we always go by bus/car/boat/rail/plane/air/land/sea

iii) meals:

when do you have breakfast?

can you meet me before lunch?

buy some smoked haddock for tea, will you?

But if a specific occasion is referred to, the article is used. Thus there is a considerable difference between saying:

I enjoy lunch
and:
I am enjoying the lunch

The first sentence refers to the enjoyment of eating regularly at midday. The second sentence refers to a specific meal.

iv) times of the day and night after prepositions other than **in** and **during**:

I don't like going out at night

these animals can often be seen after dusk

they go to bed around midnight

but:

see you in the morning!

if you feel peckish during the day, have an apple

v) seasons, especially if the noun refers to characteristics contrasting with those of the other seasons rather than to a specific timespan. Thus:

spring is here! (ie winter is over)

it's like winter today

but:

the winter was spent at expensive ski resorts

he needed the summer to recover

After **in** the definite article is sometimes used, sometimes not, with little difference in meaning:

most leaves turn yellow in (the) autumn

American English prefers to include **the** in such uses.

vi) in the combinations **next/last** + time reference:

If such combinations are seen in relation to the present, the article is not normally used:

can we meet next week?

he got drunk last night

Elsewhere the article is normal:

we arrived on March 31st and the next day was spent relaxing by the pool

they used to meet in secret; the last time they met they had been particularly careful

vii) with abstract nouns:

a talk about politics

a study of human relationships

suspicion is a terrible thing

But, of course, where the word is used in a defining sense (see 2 d) above) the article is used:

the politics of disarmament

viii) with a number of words for illnesses:

he has diabetes

I've got jaundice

However with a number of commoner illnesses the article can be used in rather more colloquial English:

she has (the) flu

he's got (the) measles

f) The definite article is not normally used when referring to place names or names of countries:

> **in France**
> **to America**

i) but there are exceptions, for example:

> **the Yemen**
> **(the) Sudan**
> **(the) Lebanon**

and where the name of a country includes a defining word:

> **the People's Republic of China**
> **the Republic of Ireland**

as well as the special case:

> **the Hague**

ii) plural place names take the article:

> **the Philippines, the Shetlands, the Azores, the Midlands, the Borders, the Netherlands, the United States**

as do names of families:

> **the Smiths**

iii) rivers and oceans take the article:

> **the Thames, the Danube, the Pacific, the Atlantic**

iv) regions take the article:

> **the Tyrol, the Ruhr, the Orient, the Crimea, the City (of London), the East End, the West End**

v) names of mountains and lakes do not take the article:

> **Ben Nevis**
> **K2**
> **Lake Michigan**

although mountain ranges do:

the Himalayas

the Alps

and there are some exceptions:

the Matterhorn

the Eiger

vi) names of streets, parks, squares etc normally do not take the article:

he lives in Wilton Street

they met in Hyde Park

there was a concert in George Square

But there are exceptions. Sometimes the article has become an actual part of the name:

the Strand

and sometimes exceptions are purely a question of local custom:

the Edgware Road

g) Names of hotels, pubs, restaurants, theatres, cinemas, museums normally take **the**:

the Caledonian (Hotel), the Red Lion, the Copper Kettle, the Old Vic, the Odeon, the Tate (Gallery)

but note **Covent Garden** (= The Royal Opera House) and **Drury Lane** (a West End theatre).

h) Newspapers and a few magazines take **the**:

the Observer, the Independent, the Daily Star

and, for instance, the magazines:

the Spectator, the Economist

However, most magazines do not take the article:

Woman's Own, **Punch**, **Private Eye** etc

and the two common TV and radio magazines, which used to be **The Radio Times** and **The TV Times** (and still are to some speakers), are now always advertised on television as:

Radio Times and **TV Times**

i) *Musical instruments*

The definite article is used in contexts such as:

she plays the clarinet

where a general skill is referred to. Note however:

in this piece he plays bass guitar

where the reference is to a specific occasion rather than a general ability.

j) Omission of the definite article for special effect:

i) The definite article is sometimes omitted for special effect - to imply a special importance, status, or sometimes just as jargon:

all pupils will assemble in hall

the number of delegates at conference

if PSBR (= public sector borrowing requirement) goes any higher . . .

ii) newspaper headlines (omission of indefinite article also):

Attempt To Break Record Fails

New Conference Centre Planned

iii) instructions (omission of indefinite article also):

break glass in emergency

3. NOUNS

A. TYPES

1 CONCRETE AND ABSTRACT NOUNS

Nouns can be classified in a number of ways. One is to divide them into (1) 'concrete' nouns, ie nouns that refer to physical beings or objects (**woman, cat, stone**) and (2) 'abstract' nouns, ie nouns that express non-physical concepts, characteristics or actions (**love, ugliness, classification**).

Many abstract nouns have been formed by adding an ending (suffix) to an adjective, noun or verb; but there are plenty of abstract nouns without such endings, eg **love, hate, concept**. Here are some common endings for abstract nouns (some of them can be used for concrete nouns too):

a) *Abstract nouns formed from other nouns*

-age	**percent+ -age**	**percentage**
-cy	**democrat+ -cy**	**democracy**
-dom	**martyr+ -dom**	**martyrdom**
-hood	**child+ -hood**	**childhood**
-ism	**alcohol+ -ism**	**alcoholism**
-ry	**chemist+ -ry**	**chemistry**

b) *Abstract nouns formed from adjectives*

-age	**short+ -age**	**shortage**
-cy	**bankrupt+ -cy**	**bankruptcy**
	normal+ -cy	**normalcy** (American English)
-hood	**likely+ -hood**	**likelihood**
-ism	**social+ -ism**	**socialism**
-ity	**normal+ -ity**	**normality**
-ness	**kind+ -ness**	**kindness**

c) *Abstract nouns formed from verbs*

-age	break+ -age	breakage
-al	arrive+ -al	arrival
-ance	utter+ -ance	utterance
-(at)ion	starve+ -ation	starvation
	operate+ -ion	operation
-ing	for the **gerund** see p 145	
-ment	treat+ -ment	treatment

Note that sometimes the ending of the noun, adjective or verb has to be changed before the suffix is added.

2   COMMON NOUNS AND PROPER NOUNS

We can also classify nouns into 'common' nouns and 'proper' nouns, the latter being names (personal and geographical) and calendar nouns, with a capital letter.

common	*proper*
cup	Peter
palace	China
cheese	Wednesday
time	August
love	Christmas

3   COUNTABLE AND UNCOUNTABLE NOUNS

A classification that is particularly relevant for the presence or absence of the indefinite article divides nouns into 'countable' and 'uncountable'. A fully countable noun can, of course, be counted (ie have a number in front of it) and therefore must have a singular as well as a plural form. Fully uncountable nouns, on the other hand, are neither singular nor plural since, by definition, they cannot be counted, though they take a singular verb. Instead we talk of such nouns as being 'mass':

countable	*uncountable*
a/one pen/three pens	furniture
a/one coat/three coats	spaghetti
a/one horse/three horses	violence
a/one child/three children	news

When we want to refer to specific instances of uncountables, we have to use a phrase with a countable noun. Thus in **a piece of furniture/two pieces of furniture**, it is **piece** that is counted, not **furniture**, which remains uncountable. Similarly **a strand of spaghetti, an act of violence, an item of news**, where **strand, act** and **item** are perfectly normal countable nouns. The count-word for **cattle** is **head**, which never takes -s in this sense: **ten head of cattle**.

Other examples of fully uncountable nouns: **advice, baggage, garbage, information, luggage, rubbish**. For a word like **knowledge**, see b) v below. For **accommodation**, see f) below.

a) *Nouns that can be either countable or uncountable*

i) Some nouns can either be countable or uncountable, depending on whether the meaning is 'individual' or 'mass'. Such nouns frequently refer to food or material:

countable	*uncountable*
that sheep has only one lamb	we had lamb for dinner
what lovely strawberries	there's too much strawberry in this ice cream
do you like my nylons? (nylon stockings)	most socks contain nylon
he bought a paper (newspaper)	I'd like some writing paper
she's a beauty	love beauty and truth
she has a lovely voice	she has little voice in the making of decisions

ii) Uncountable nouns are often made countable when 'a portion of' or 'a type of' is understood:

I'd like a coffee (a cup of coffee)
two white wines, please (two glasses of white wine)
Britain has a large selection of cheeses (types of cheese)
a very good beer (type of beer)

iii) A few uncountable nouns are sometimes used in the plural to indicate vastness, normally in literary style:

The Snows of Kilimanjaro (a story by Hemingway)
still waters run deep (proverb)

Waters is, however, perfectly normal when it refers to the sea area close to a country (**the territorial limit of Danish waters**) and when it has a medicinal meaning (**he has been to take the waters at Lourdes**).

Weather is 'mass' except in the phrase **in all weathers**.

b) *Countability: some problems*

Some nouns are neither fully countable nor fully uncountable. A noun that is fully countable can be preceded by the indefinite article or any numeral or any plural pronoun (eg **these**) or plural quantifier (**few, many**) and can take a plural verb:

a/one goat
three/these/those/few/many goats are . . .

i) But what about a word like **data** (from the Latin **datum** (sg.), **data** (pl.))? We can say **these/those data are** but not everybody feels happy with **many/few data** (preferring **much/little data**) and **seven data** is unacceptable: you can't count **data**, which also means it does not have a singular, ie **a datum** does not exist (except in certain very specialized types of professional jargon). Since the word, despite its Latin plural ending and despite its possible combination with **these/those** and a plural verb, is not countable, it is not surprising that it is rapidly in the process of moving to the camp of uncountables: **this/that/much/little data is** is now heard (and often written) more frequently than **these/those/many/few data are**.

ii) Consider also a word like **damages** 'money to be paid for causing damage' as in:

Dentist Donald Ritchie is contesting the amount of damages

Note that **amount** is normally used with uncountables (**a large amount of butter**) whereas **number** is preferred with countables (**a large number of students**). Here we find **amount** used with **damages**, which, judging by its ending, is plural. But how plural is its meaning? How countable is it? It isn't countable at all, and that is why **amount** cannot be replaced by **number** in the sentence quoted above. Similarly **many damages** is impossible. We say **much damages** or rephrase the sentence to **... much in the way of damages/... a lot in damages**.

iii) We can't say **many damages** but we can say, for instance, **many vegetables** (and **a/one vegetable**). However, **much vegetables** sometimes competes with **many vegetables** when countability is not of the essence:

the Japanese still eat twice as much vegetables, including beans, as the British

Much was preferred by the writer of that sentence to **many** because he felt **many** to be too individualizing: **many vegetables** would tend to mean **many kinds of vegetables**, which is not what is meant at all. The writer had 'quantity' or 'amount' in mind. He could, of course, have avoided the problem by writing **a lot of vegetables**; but the point still remains that the occasional use of **much** with certain plural nouns shows clearly that they are thought of as 'mass'.

Many people would find such sentences unacceptable, but they are far too frequent (especially in spoken English) to be dismissed merely as slips of the tongue (or, occasionally, the pen).

iv) There is a problem with 'mass' modifiers such as **little, less, much, amount (of)** and plural nouns, the most common of these 'mass' modifiers being **less**. Many speakers today hardly make use of the word **fewer**; and whether we like it or not, the most widespread comparative of **few** in spoken (and often in written) English is **less**. **Fewer** tends to be formal or overprecise, and it is perfectly normal to hear phrases like **less books, less students, less crimes,** spoken by the educated and less educated alike.

v) indefinite article and plurals with uncountable nouns:

Some abstract nouns are fully countable (**possibility**) and some are normally fully uncountable (**indignation, hate, anger**). But some of these abstract uncountables often take the indefinite article, especially if accompanied by an adjective or an adjectival structure, such as a prepositional phrase or relative clause. This is because the adjectival element *singles out* or individualizes:

candidates must have a good knowledge of English

he expressed an indignation so intense that people were taken aback

Such abstract nouns can sometimes be found in the plural. **Fears** and **doubts** are frequent:

he expressed his fears

I have my doubts

In other cases such plurals denote individual manifestations of the abstract concept:

the use of too many adjectives is one of his stylistic infelicities,

and certain instances are deliberately literary:

such highly self-conscious vaguenesses of expression

c) *Nouns in -ics*

When these are considered abstract concepts, they take a singular verb:

mathematics is a difficult subject

whereas a plural verb and plural modifier are preferred when practical manifestations of the concept are emphasized:

his mathematics are very poor (his calculations)

what are your politics? (political views)

Other words of this kind include **acoustics, athletics, linguistics**.

d) *Diseases, games and news*

Some nouns that end in what looks like a plural -s are uncountable. These are **news**, the 'disease' words **measles, mumps, rickets, shingles** and a few 'games' words:

the news hasn't arrived yet

mumps is not a dangerous disease

darts is still played in many pubs

billiards is preferred to snooker in some countries

Similarly **bowls, draughts, dominoes** and the American **checkers**.

e) *'Pair' words*

Certain plural nouns referring to things consisting of two equal parts have no singular form and must be preceded by **a pair of** if we wish to emphasize countability:

my trousers are here

this is a good pair of trousers

two new pairs of trousers

similarly:

**bellows, binoculars,
glasses** (spectacles), **knickers
pants, pincers, pliers,
pyjamas** (**pajamas** in American English)
**scales, scissors, shears,
shorts, spectacles, tights,
tongs, tweezers**.

f) *Nouns that normally occur in the plural only and take a*
plural verb:

i)   **arms** (weapons),
    arrears, auspices, banns,
    clothes,
    customs (foreign goods tax),
    dregs, earnings, entrails,
    goods, greens (vegetables),
    guts (entrails; courage),
    lodgings, looks (appearance),
    manners (behaviour),
    means (wealth),
    odds, outskirts,
    pains (trouble, effort),
    premises (place),
    quarters (lodgings), **remains,**
    riches, savings,
    spirits (mood; liquor),
    (soap) suds, surroundings,
    tropics, valuables,
and the Italian plural **graffiti** (which is also used with a
singular verb).

Such nouns normally take a plural verb but sometimes
have a singular form as well, often with a change of
meaning:

ashes (in general) but **cigar(ette) ash, tobacco ash**

contents 'what is contained' but **content** 'the amount
contained', eg:
show me the contents of your purse
but:
what exactly is the lead content of petrol?

funds 'ready money' but **fund** 'money source', eg:
I'm short of funds
but:
**the church fund does not hold enough money for the
repairs**

stairs: commoner than **stair** in the sense 'flight of
stairs'. **Stair** can also refer to a step in a flight of stairs.

thanks: note the possibility of using the indefinite article before an adjective (no singular here):

a very special thanks to ...

wages: often in the singular also, especially when preceded by an adjective:

all we want is a decent wage

Accommodations (place to live) is American English. British English uses **accommodation** as an uncountable 'mass' noun.

ii) A few nouns have no plural ending:

cattle, clergy, livestock, police, vermin

but even **clergy** and **police** can occasionally take the indefinite article if modified by an adjective, prepositional phrase or relative clause. In such cases there is an important change of meaning from 'clergymen' and 'policemen' to '**body** of clergymen' and 'police **force**'. Compare:

seventy-five clergy were present

the problem is whether the country needs a clergy with such old-fashioned views

at least thirty police were needed for that task

the countryside needed a semi-military police

Folk in the sense of 'people, persons' is normally without -s in British English:

some folk just don't know how to behave

whereas American English prefers **folks**, which in British English is normally reserved for familiar address and the sense 'family, parents':

sit down, folks

I'd like you to meet my folks

Youth (young generation) can be followed by a singular as well as a plural verb:

our country's youth has/have little to look forward to

but the word is fully countable in the sense 'young man':

they arrested a youth/two youths

g) *Collective nouns*

i) These are nouns that in the singular sometimes take a singular verb, sometimes a plural one. The choice depends on whether the noun is used to express group collectivity or emphasizes the individuals of the group:

the jury is one of the safeguards of our legal system

the jury have returned their verdict

Note **their** in the second example. Pronouns referring to such nouns normally agree in number with the verb:

as the crowd moves forward it becomes visible on the hill-top

the crowd have been protesting for hours; they are getting very impatient

The use of a plural verb is more widespread in British English than in American.

The following are typical examples of collective nouns:

**army, audience, choir, chorus,
class, committee, enemy,
family, firm, gang,
(younger and older) generation,
government, group,
majority, minority, orchestra,
Parliament, proletariat, public, team.**

National proper nouns referring to a (sports) team normally take a plural verb in British English:

Germany have beaten England

although both singular and plural are possible.

ii) Note that national names in the plural behave like collective nouns:

the Philippines has its problems like any other country

the Philippines consist of a group of very beautiful islands

Similarly **the Bahamas, the United States** etc.

iii) The words **crew, staff, people** are often collective nouns, as in:

the crew is excellent

the crew have all enjoyed themselves

the staff of that school has a good record

the staff don't always behave themselves

it is difficult to imagine a people that has suffered more

the people have not voted against the re-introduction of hanging

These three words differ from other collective nouns in that they can be fully countable with or without a plural -s, depending on meaning. If they have -s, the plural is simply like all -s plurals of other collective nouns:

five crews/staffs/peoples (nations)/armies/governments etc

But without the -s, the plural refers to individual members:

the captain had to manage with only fifteen crew

the English Department had to get rid of five staff

he spoke to six people about it

It is, of course, perfectly normal to speak instead of **crew members, staff members** or **members of staff**.

For **clergy** and **police**, see f) ii above.

B.   FORMS

1   PLURALS IN -(E)S

a)   The normal plural of English nouns ends in -(e)s:

soup: soups	bush: bushes
peg: pegs	match: matches
bus : buses	page: pages
quiz: quizzes	box: boxes

-es is used for words ending in -s, -x, -z, -ch or -sh.

b)   Nouns ending in a consonant plus -y change the -y to -ies:

lady: ladies   **loony: loonies**

But the regular -s plural is used when the -y is preceded by a vowel:

trolley: trolleys

One exception to this is the formal or legal usage **monies** (from **money**):

all monies currently payable to the society

For more on this see the section **Spelling**, p 247.

c)   Nouns in -o sometimes have -s, sometimes -es in the plural. It is difficult to establish any hard and fast rules here except to say that only -s is added if (1) the -o follows another vowel (**embryo: embryos, studio: studios**) or (2) if the noun is an abbreviation (**photo: photos, piano: pianos (from pianoforte)**). In other cases it is difficult to generalize although we may perhaps notice a tendency to -s with words that are still felt to be rather foreign:

(with -es) echo, cargo, hero, mosquito, negro, potato, tomato, torpedo

(with -s) canto, memento, proviso, quarto, solo, zero, zoo

(with -s or -es) banjo, buffalo, commando, flamingo, motto, volcano

d) Some nouns in -**f(e)** change the -**f** to -**ve** in the plural:

calf: calves

Similarly: **elf, half, knife, leaf, life, loaf, self, sheaf, shelf, thief, wife, wolf**

Some can take either -**ves** or -**s**:

dwarf: dwarfs/dwarves   **scarf: scarfs/scarves**

hoof: hoofs/hooves   **wharf: wharfs/wharves**

and a large number keep the -**f**:

belief: beliefs

Similarly: **chief, cliff, proof, roof, safe, sniff** etc

e) A few French words ending in an unpronounced -**s** in the singular have an unchanged written plural form, but /z/ is added to the plural in speech:

corps — the plural is pronounced to rhyme with 'cause'

f) French words in -**eu** or -**eau** may add -**s** or -**x** (both pronounced /z/), eg:

adieu, bureau, tableau

gateau normally adds -**x**.

g) *Animal names*

Some animal names, especially those of fish, behave (or nearly always behave) like the nouns under 3a) below, ie they do not take a plural ending:

cod, hake, herring, mackerel, pike, salmon, trout (but **sharks**); **deer, sheep; grouse**

while others vary between -**s** or nothing, often depending on whether they occur in a hunting context, in which case the -**s** is often dropped. Compare:

these graceful antelopes have just been bought by the zoo

they went to Africa to shoot antelope

Similarly:

> **buffalo, giraffe, lion; duck, fowl, partridge, pheasant**

and many others.

The normal plural of **fish** is **fish**, but **fishes** is used to refer to 'kinds of fish'.

h) *Numerals*

i) **hundred, thousand, million, dozen, score** and **gross** have no plural -s when preceded by another numeral:

> **five hundred/thousand/million people**
>
> **two dozen eggs**
>
> **we'll order three gross**

but

> **there were hundreds/thousands/millions of them**
>
> **I've told you dozens of times**
>
> **Peter and Kate have scores of friends**

ii) the measurement words **foot** and **pound** can take either a plural or a singular form:

> **Kate is five foot/feet eight**
>
> **that comes to three pound(s) fifty**

2   PLURALS BY VOWEL CHANGE

There is a small group of words for which the plural form involves vowel change:

> **foot: feet**
>
> **goose: geese**
>
> **louse: lice**
>
> **man: men**
>
> **mouse: mice**
>
> **tooth: teeth**
>
> **woman: women** /wɪmɪn/

3   ZERO PLURALS

a)   *singular and plural both without -s*

(air)craft, **counsel** (lawyer), **offspring**, **quid**, eg:

we saw a few aircraft

both counsel asked for an adjournment

this will cost you ten quid (colloquial = pound(s))

See also g) above.

(Mass) media (radio, television, newspapers) sometimes takes a singular verb, sometimes a plural one, without any difference in meaning.

The words **kind, sort, type** when occurring in the phrase **these/those** + noun + **of** frequently omit the -s:

these kind of people always complain

she always buys those sort of records

It is also possible to say:

this kind of record

with both nouns in the singular.

b)   *singular and plural both with -s*

barracks, **crossroads**, **innings**, **means** (= method, compare **means** = wealth on p 36), **gallows**, **headquarters**, **series**, **shambles**, **species**, **-works** (factory), eg:

every means was tried to improve matters

this is a dreadful shambles

they have built a new gasworks north of here

Some of these nouns, especially **barracks**, **gallows**, **headquarters**, **-works** can also be used in a singular sense with a plural verb:

these are the new steelworks

when reference is made to one factory only.

c) *dice and pence*

These are, strictly speaking, irregular plurals from **die** and **penny**, but are rapidly replacing them as new singulars.

Die is hardly ever used except in fossilized expressions such as **the die is cast** or **straight as a die**. And it is now normal to hear **one pence** rather than **one penny** with reference to cost; but the coin itself can still be referred to as **a penny** and several of them as **pennies**, as in **these are 18th-century pennies**. Like **die**, **penny** has become fossilized in certain phrases, eg **to spend a penny** (go to the toilet).

4   PLURALS IN -EN

There are just three of these, and only one:

child: children

is common. The other two are:

ox: oxen   **brother: brethren**

the latter referring mainly to members of religious groups or associations, as in:

the Protestants found warm hospitality among their Catholic brethren

The normal plural of **brother** is, of course, **brothers**.

5   PLURALS IN -A OR -S

These are Latin words in singular -um or Greek words in singular -on. Many of these have plural -s, especially if they are in common use, eg:

museum, stadium, demon, electron

Some, often learned, words usually change -um/-on to -a, eg:

an addendum   **numerous addenda**

Similarly:

bacterium, curriculum, erratum, ovum, criterion, phenomenon

Some vary between the -s and the -a plural form:

memorandum, millennium, symposium, automaton

The plural of **medium** is always **mediums** when the word refers to clairvoyants; when it means 'method', the plural can be either **media** or **mediums**. For **(mass) media**, see **Zero Plurals** above, p 43. For **data**, see p 32.

There are signs that **strata** (the plural of **stratum**) may soon replace **stratum** as a new singular.

6 PLURALS IN -E OR -S

These words are Latin and Greek and end in **-a** in the singular. Those in frequent use have **-s**, such as **arena** and **drama**. The more technical or scientific words tend to add **-e** (the resulting **-ae** being pronounced /iː/ or /aɪ/), eg **alumna** and **larva**. Some take either ending depending on how 'academic' the context is. Thus **antenna** always adds **-e** when it refers to insects, but **-s** as the American word for aerial. Similarly, **formula** and **vertebra**.

7 PLURALS IN -I OR -S (Italian words)

A few words from Italian, notably **libretto, tempo** and **virtuoso**, sometimes preserve their Italian plural in **-i**/iː/, especially **tempo**. Sometimes they take the English **-s**. Note that **confetti** and the pastas **macaroni, ravioli, spaghetti** and others are uncountable mass-words, ie they take singular verbs. For **graffiti**, see p 36.

8 PLURALS IN -I OR -ES (Latin words)

Those that are common normally take plural **-es**, such as:

campus, chorus, virus

Those felt to be rather learned are more likely to keep their Latin plural **-i** (pronounced /iː/ or /aɪ/), eg:

alumnus, bacillus, stimulus.

And there are those that take either, eg **cactus, fungus, nucleus, syllabus** — and the latinized Greek words **hippopotamus** and **papyrus**. The plural of **genius** is

geniuses in the sense of 'highly intelligent person' but **genii** when it means 'guardian spirit'.

9   PLURALS OF NOUNS IN -EX OR -IX

These Latin words may retain their foreign plural by changing **-ex/-ix** to **-ices**, or they may just add **-es**, eg:

index: plural **indices** or **indexes**

Similarly, **appendix**, **matrix**, **vortex**

But note that **appendixes** is the only plural for the body organ, whereas both **appendixes** and **appendices** can be used for parts of a book or thesis.

10   THE PLURAL OF GREEK NOUNS IN -IS

These change **-is** /ɪs/ to **-es** /iːz/ in the plural, eg:

an analysis   **various different analyses**

Similarly:

axis, basis, crisis, diagnosis, hypothesis, oasis, parenthesis, synopsis, thesis

But note: **metropolis: metropolises**

11   PLURALS IN -IM OR -S

The three Hebrew words **kibbutz**, **cherub** and **seraph** may take either **-(e)s** (normal) or **-im** in the plural.

12   PLURALS OF COMPOUNDS

a)   *Plural of the second element*

This is normal when the second element is a noun (not preceded by a preposition):

boy scouts, football hooligans, girl friends, road users, man-eaters (compare **menservants** in c) below)

and when the compound consists of verb + adverb:

lay-bys, lie-ins, sit-ins, stand-bys, tip-offs

Note that measures in **-ful** can have the **-s** on either element: **spoonfuls** or **spoonsful**.

b) *Plural of the first element*

This is normal if the second element is a prepositional phrase:

editors-in-chief, fathers-in-law, men-of-war, aides-de-camp

But if the first element is not considered an individual, final **-s** is normal, as in:

will-o'-the-wisps; jack-in-the-boxes

Compounds consisting of a noun formed from a verb and an adverb also add **-s** to the first element (as opposed to those consisting of verb + adverb, which add final **-s**; see a) above):

carryings-on, hangers-on, passers-by

Compounds in **-to-be** add **-s** to the first element:

brides-to-be, mothers-to-be

First-element plurals are also found if the second element is an adjective:

Lords temporal and spiritual

But many of these vary with the second-element plurals increasingly used:

attorneys general or **attorney generals**

directors general or **director generals**

poets laureate or **poet laureates**

courts-martial or **court-martials**

c) *Plural of both elements*

This is possible if compounds with **man** or **woman** refer to the sexes (but the first element can also be singular):

menservants (compare **man-eaters** in a) above)

gentlemen farmers

women doctors

C.   USE: PLURAL VERSUS SINGULAR

a)   *The distributive plural*

   i)   type 1, in a phrase:

   Instead of repeating a singular noun as in:

   page seven and page eight

   we can say:

   pages seven and eight

   In such cases many languages would use only the singular (**page seven and eight**) but English prefers the plural:

   between the ages of 30 and 45

   the fifteenth and sixteenth centuries

   the reigns of Henry VI and Elizabeth I

   although the singular is sometimes used, especially if a plural could cause a misunderstanding. Thus we would say:

   on this and the following page

   since **pages** would mean more than two. Similarly, if each element is modified or emphasized, the singular is preferred:

   in the late 19th and early 20th century

   ii)   type 2, across a clause:

   In these cases the plural noun (often preceded by a possessive pronoun) refers to an earlier plural noun or plural pronoun, for example:

   we changed our minds

   many people are unhappy about their long noses

   cats seem to spend their lives sleeping

they deserve **a kick up their backsides**

we respectfully removed our hats

can we change places?

But there is frequent vacillation. People may be **up to their waists** or **up to the waist** in water, and **up to their necks** or **up to the neck** in both water and debt. Drivers **change gear** or **gears** and failing to do so at the right time may cause the **death** or **deaths of their passengers**. There are situations (quite a few according to the media) where people are left with **egg on their face** or **faces**, ie 'looking foolish'; but only **faces** if the egg is real! And there are things which some **turn their nose(s) up at**, ie 'consider inferior'. It seems that the more figurative the expression, the more likely the singular, sometimes preceded by the definite article rather than the possessive pronoun. Thus we **pay through the nose, take children under our wing**, and are sometimes **at the end of our tether** − examples in which a concrete image hardly presents itself.

b) *Premodification and postmodification*

When a noun is postmodified by a preposition + a plural noun, as in:

   a collection of bottles

the plural noun of the postmodification will normally change to the singular in a premodification:

   a bottle collection

There are plenty of such instances: **record dealer**, **letter box**, **foreign language teaching**.

However, there are cases where plural premodifications are preferred. Sometimes this is because the singular alternative would have different associations. Thus we would normally say:

   a problems page (a page in a newspaper or magazine dealing with people's problems) because a premodifying singular **problem** normally implies 'causing problems' or being 'problematic', as in:

> **a problem student**
> **a problem case**

Similarly, we have to say:

> **a singles bar** (bar for unmarried people)
> **an explosives investigation**

since

> **a single bar**
> **an explosive investigation**

would mean something quite different.

But often either a singular or a plural is possible:

> **in this noun(s) section**
> **a Falkland(s) hero**
> **a call for job(s) cuts**

D.   THE GENITIVE

1   FORMS

a)   The genitive singular is formed by adding -'s:

> **the cat's tail**

and the genitive plural by adding only the apostrophe to the plural:

> **the cats' tails**

There is often confusion about the position of the apostrophe. Compare these two examples:

> **the boy's school**
> **the boys' school**

In the first **boy** is a singular noun, so we are talking about the school which one boy goes to. In the second the noun is **boys**, a plural, so we are talking about the school which several boys go to.

If the plural does not end in -s, the genitive plural has -'s like the singular:

> **the men's toilet   the children's room**

b) *Exceptions:*

 i) Many classical (especially Greek) names in -s normally add just the apostrophe, particularly if they have more than one syllable:

> **Socrates' wife, Aeschylus' plays**

 We may even find non-classical names treated in this way, as in:

> **Dickens' (or Dickens's) novels**

 ii) Before **sake** the genitive singular is normally marked only by the apostrophe in nouns ending in -s:

> **for politeness' sake**

c) The compound-noun types mentioned on p 46 add the genitive -'s to the second element even if the plural -s is added to the first, for example:

> **she summoned her ladies-in-waiting**

> **the lady-in-waiting's mistress**

In the plural it is more normal to use the **of**-construction:

> **the request of the ladies-in-waiting**

2 THE GENITIVE VERSUS THE OF-CONSTRUCTION

a) *Animates (people, animals)*

The genitive is more common with persons than non-persons:

> **John's mind   my mother's ring**

Of is not normally used in these two examples.

But with reference to animals either is possible:

> **the wings of an insect/the insect's wings**
>
> **the movements of the worm/the worm's movements**

However, higher animals are treated in this respect like persons:

> **the lion's paw shot out from the cage**

b) *Inanimates (things)*

The normal construction is with **of**:

> **the size of the coat**
>
> **the colour of the telephone**

But with certain inanimate nouns **-'s** is also possible:

> **the mind's ability to recover**
>
> **the poem's capacity to move**

especially if such nouns refer to places or institutions:

> **England's heritage** (= the heritage of England)
>
> **the University's catering facilities** (= the catering facilities of the University)

Nouns referring to measurements of time and value make frequent use of the genitive:

> **a whole night's journey**
>
> **today's menu**
>
> **two months' work**
>
> **you have had your pound's worth**

Note that the **of**-construction with nouns referring to time often implies top quality or special selection, as in:

> **our actor of the year award goes to . . .**

or it may imply that the time-span is not to be taken literally, as in:

> **the University of tomorrow**

where **tomorrow** can only mean 'the future'.

A genitive can have either literal or metaphorical reference:

Tomorrow's World (metaphorical)

tomorrow's phone call (literal)

tomorrow's food (either literal or metaphorical)

Measurements of distance are sometimes in the genitive, especially in fixed or fossilized phrases:

a stone's throw (away)   **at arm's length**

3 THE GENITIVE NOT FOLLOWED BY A NOUN

a) If the noun that the genitive qualifies is clear from the context, it can be left out:

it's not my father's car, it's my mother's

b) The so-called 'double genitive' (ie **of**-construction **and** genitive in the same phrase) is frequent if the genitive refers to a *definite* person. But the first noun is normally preceded by the **indefinite** article, an **indefinite** pronoun or a numeral:

he's a friend of Peter's

he's an acquaintance of my father's

he's no uncle of Mrs Pitt's

here are some relatives of Miss Young's

two sisters of my mother's came to visit

Occasionally a demonstrative pronoun can precede the first noun. Such instances imply a certain degree of familiarity:

that car of your father's − how much does he want for it?

The definite article cannot normally be used with the first noun unless a relative clause (or equivalent modification) follows the genitive:

the poem of Larkin's (that) we read yesterday is lovely

this is the only poem of Larkin's to have moved me

c) The noun understood after a genitive often refers to premises of some kind:

> **at the baker's** (= baker's shop)
>
> **at Mary's** (= at Mary's place)

It is worth noting that if a (business) establishment is particularly well known, the apostrophe is often omitted. Thus we would tend to write **at Smiths** or **in Harrods**, the former being a chain of shops all over Britain, and the latter a famous London store. But we would usually find eg **he bought it at Bruce Miller's** since that music shop has not imprinted itself very firmly on the collective mind of the nation.

4   THE GROUP GENITIVE

The 'group genitive' refers to two kinds of construction: (1) noun + prepositional modifier and (2) nouns connected by **and**. In such combinations it is possible to add the **-'s** to the last element:

> **the Queen of Holland's yacht**
>
> **the head of department's office**
>
> **John and Kate's new house**
>
> **an hour and a half's work**

In the plural an **of**-construction is more normal:

> **the regalia of the Queens of Holland**

However, if the two nouns do not form a unit, each of them takes the **-'s**:

> **Shakespeare's and Marlowe's plays**

E.   FEMININES

In English it is common not to use a special word or ending to distinguish the sex of a noun. Many nouns refer to both male and female:

> **artist, banker, cousin, friend, lawyer, neighbour, novelist, teacher, zoologist**

But it is sometimes possible to use endings to distinguish male and female:

feminine	*masculine*
actress	**actor**
duchess	**duke**
goddess	**god**
heroine	**hero**
princess	**prince**
widow	**widower**
businesswoman	**businessman**

although in many cases the distinction can be seen as parallel to that between the different *words* **daughter/son**, **cow/bull** etc. It is quite possible to say **she is a good actor** or **she was the hero of the day**.

If it is necessary to identify a person's sex, use either:

a female friend	**a male friend**
a female student	**a male student**

or:

a woman doctor	**a man doctor**

For the plural of such combinations, see p 47.

When it is not necessary or possible to distinguish or identify a person's sex it is common to use the word **person**:

a chairperson

a salesperson

a spokesperson

although some women are quite happy being **chairmen** or being addressed as **Madam Chairman**.

Use of the word **person** is becoming increasingly common, for example in job advertisements:

security person required

4. ADJECTIVES

A. TYPES

A useful distinction is made between (1) those adjectives that are always 'attributive' (ie bound to a following noun), (2) those that are always 'predicative' (those that function as subject complement after a noun), and (3) those that can be either. See further p 58.

Another related division is into 'gradable' and 'non-gradable' (see further p 62).

B. FORMS

1 COMPARISON

a) There are three degrees of comparison: **absolute**, **comparative** and **superlative**:

sweet	**beautiful**	(absolute)
sweeter	**more beautiful**	(comparative)
sweetest	**the most beautiful**	(superlative)

For spelling changes resulting from the addition of -er, -est (eg **happy** – **happier** or **big** – **bigger**) see p 247.

b) *-er/-est or more/most?*

   i) The shorter the adjective, the more likely it is to form the comparative and superlative by adding -er and -est. This applies especially to those of one syllable, such as **keen**, **fine**, **late**, **wide**, **neat** etc. Very common adjectives such as **big** or **fast** will always take the -er/-est form.

   If adjectives have two syllables, there is considerable variation between -er/-est and **more/most**, -er/-est

being particularly common with adjectives ending in **-y,
-le, -ow, -er**:

(noisy) **this is the noisiest pub I've been in**

(feeble) **this is the feeblest excuse I've heard**

(shallow) **the stream is shallower up there**

(clever) **she's the cleverest**

The tendency is for **more** and **most** to become more
widespread at the expense of **-er/-est**. **Commoner** and
pleasanter used to be more common than they are now;
so did **politer** and **handsomer** as opposed to **more
polite** and **more handsome**, which are now normal.

ii) Adjectives of more than two syllables use **more** and **the
most**:

this is the most idiotic thing I ever heard!

I prefer a more traditional Christmas

he's getting more and more predictable

But there are exceptions to this:

she's unhappier than she has ever been

he's got the untidiest room in the whole house

But in these cases the forms with **more/most** can also
be used.

iii) Adjectives which are formed from past participles form
the comparative and superlative with **more/the most**:

she's more gifted than her sister

the most advanced students

that's the most bored I've ever been!

Tired can take the **-er/-est** endings.

iv) If two adjectives are compared, then we can only use
more:

this sauce is more sweet than sour

2 IRREGULAR COMPARISON

A few adjectives have irregular comparatives and superlatives:

bad	worse	worst
far	further/farther	furthest/farthest
good	better	best
little	less/lesser	least
many	more	most
much	more	most

Note also **late, latter, last** (besides **later, latest**) and **old, elder, eldest** (besides **older, oldest**).

For the usage of comparatives and superlatives (including variants), see p 62.

3 NEGATIVE COMPARISON

To form comparatives 'in a negative direction' the adverbs **less/the least** are placed before the adjective:

it's less interesting than I thought it would be

this was the least interesting of his comments

As an alternative for the comparative:

it's not as/so interesting as I thought it would be

C. USE

1 ATTRIBUTIVE AND PREDICATIVE

a) The terms 'attributive' and 'predicative' refer to the position of the adjective. If it is before the noun, it is attributive (**this old car**). If it is on its own after a verb, it is predicative (**this car is old**).

b) We can divide adjectives into those that can be attributive *and* predicative (like **old** above); those that can be attributive only, like **utter** (**this is utter nonsense**); and those that can be predicative only, like **afraid** (**the girl is afraid**). Where an adjective has more than one meaning, these meanings may fall into different categories.

c) *Attributive only*

i) Whether an adjective can be attributive only, predicative only, or either, depends on its meaning. If it can be either, it tends to characterize its noun directly:

can you lift that heavy stone?

that stone is heavy

If it is attributive only, it does not describe its noun in the same way:

he is a heavy drinker

This sentence does not refer to the drinker's weight. It is equivalent to **he drinks heavily**. In other words, **heavy** is here semi-adverbial in meaning, qualifying a strong verb-element in the noun. Such adjectives cannot be used predicatively. Other examples of this are:

he's a late developer   **she's a messy eater**

are you an early riser?

Such nouns cannot be used without adjectives. However, if the noun in **-er** has become a fully established word in the language in the sense that it is not dependent on an attributive adjective with adverbial force, having lost some of its verb-like character, then the adjective (when present) may be either attributive or predicative:

he's a good teacher   **he's an excellent baker**

this teacher is good   **this baker is excellent**

Some nouns, for instance **worker**, may function either like **teacher** or **baker**:

they are fast workers   **these workers are fast**

or like **developer** and **riser**, as in the idiomatic phrase:

you're a fast worker, aren't you?

which refers to somebody trying hard to gain the sexual favours of a woman.

ii) Other kinds of purely attributive adjectives include quite a few that are used mainly for intensification:

(a) **a pure colour/the colours are pure**

(b) **I met her by pure chance**

In (a) **pure** is an ordinary characterizing adjective and can therefore be both attributive and predicative. In (b) **pure** is an intensifier and cannot be used predicatively. Similarly:

that was a perfect meal/the meal was perfect

but

he's a perfect stranger to me

not

this stranger is perfect to me

iii) Adjectives that are purely categorizing rather than descriptive are normally attributive only:

(a) **he has a very musical sense of rhythm**

(b) **this metal rod is, in fact, a musical instrument**

In (a) **musical** is descriptive; in (b) it is categorizing, referring to a category, or kind, of instrument. We can therefore say **his sense of rhythm is very musical** but not **this instrument is very musical**. Similarly, there is considerable difference between **little** in:

he's got a funny thumb and little finger (categorizing)

this ring is too big for such a little finger (descriptive)

Only **little** as used in the second example can be predicative.

iv) Certain adjectives that have a strong affinity with their corresponding noun phrases in fixed constructions are attributive only, as in:

he's a natural scientist

This does not mean that he is the opposite of an unnatural scientist (whatever that may mean). **Natural**

scientist has here been formed from **natural science**, which is a certain branch of science. Similarly, **classical linguist** is somebody who studies **classical languages**. Past participles are sometimes used in this way:

a disabled toilet (toilet for disabled people)

d) *Predicative only*

Adjectives that can be predicative only normally refer to a physical condition or mental state, such as **afraid**, **ashamed**, **faint** (= about to fall unconscious), **fond**, **loath**, **poorly**, **(un)well**:

the girl is afraid

the children need not feel ashamed

my uncle is fond of me

my family would be loath to help you out

the singer suddenly felt faint

our mother is poorly and has been unwell for some time

But note the set expression:

he's not a well man

Similarly, **ill** and **glad** are normally predicative, but are occasionally attributive when they do not refer to people:

my aunt is very ill

the doctor was glad to receive the message

his ill health may explain his ill humour

these are glad tidings

The physical conditions or mental states similar to those referred to above can sometimes be expressed attributively by other words:

she's a frightened girl (compare **afraid**)

she has always been an unwilling helper (compare **loath**)

she's a happy person (compare **glad**)

he's a sick man (compare **ill**)

e) *Gradable versus non-gradable*

Gradable adjectives can form comparatives and superlatives, and be preceded by a qualifying adverb:

she is bigger than you   **she is very big**

Most adjectives that can be used predicatively are also gradable, but those that can be used attributively only (see above) are not. We can say **a social worker** (meaning somebody who does social work) but not **a more social worker** or **an extremely social worker**. We can say that something is **sheer madness**, but not that it is **sheerer madness** than something else, nor that it is **incredibly sheer madness**. This is because **social** (as used above) and **sheer** can only be attributive.

2   COMPARISON

a) *further/farther and furthest/farthest*

Further is more common than **farther** with reference to distance (also in adverbial usage):

this is the furthest (farthest) point

(And as an adverb: **I can't go any further (farther)**)

If the reference is to time, amount or number, only **further** is possible:

any further misdemeanours and you're out

this must be delayed until a further meeting

anything further can be discussed tomorrow

and as an adverb:

they didn't pursue the matter any further

b) *later/latter and latest/last*

Later and **latest** refer to time, **latter** and **last** to sequence:

(a) **his latest book is on war poetry**

(b) **his last book was on war poetry**

Latest in (a) means 'most recent', whereas **last** in (b) means the one at the end of a series of books.

For **latter**, see under **Numerals**, p 240. Note further **latter** implying a division into two, as in **the latter part of the century**.

c) *less/lesser*

Less is quantitative, **lesser** is qualitative:

use less butter

the lesser of two evils

you'll lose less money if you follow my plan

after further investigation he faced a lesser charge

But note **the lesser** (as opposed to **the great(er)**) as a categorizing adjective in scientific or technical language:

the Lesser Black-backed Gull (ornithological name)

For **less** in connection with the question of countability, see **Nouns**, p 33.

d) *older/elder and oldest/eldest*

Elder and **eldest** normally refer to family relationships only:

this is my elder/eldest brother

although **older** is also possible in such contexts. If **than** follows, only **older** is possible:

my brother is older than I am

Note **elder** used as a noun:

listen to your elders

she is my elder by two years

the elders of the tribe

e) The comparative is used when two people or things are compared:

of the two she is the cleverer

In everyday spoken English the superlative is also heard:

of the two she is the cleverest

except, of course, when **than** follows (**she is cleverer than her brother**).

f)   The comparative is normally used for explicit comparison, ie we know what or whom something or somebody is compared to. However, in advertising language, the comparison often remains implicit:

Greece − for a better holiday

g)   In certain cases the comparative is used not for degree, but for contrast. This is particularly true of those comparatives that have no absolute forms as adjectives:

former: latter	**inner: outer**
upper: nether	**lesser: greater** (see 2 above)

Nether has now been replaced in most cases by **lower** and is almost confined to jocular usage:

he removed his nether garments (ie trousers)

h)   The absolute superlative: this expresses 'a very high degree' rather than 'the highest degree'. Normally **most** rather than **-est** is used, even with adjectives of one syllable:

this is most kind!

your lecture was most interesting

- but sometimes **-est** is used attributively:

she was rather plain but could suddenly produce the sweetest smile

please accept my warmest congratulations!

3   POSITION

a)   If more than one adjective precedes the noun, those that can easily be predicative as well come first (eg those that tend to characterize rather than categorize). Adjectives that can take up an attributive position only are too closely linked to their nouns for another word to intervene:

he is a young parliamentary candidate

he is a sweet-natured atomic physicist

they have employed a conscientious social worker

Note how the adjectives **old** and **little** subtly change their meaning depending on position (a-d) versus (e-h):

(a) **they only have old worn-out records**

(b) **up the path came a very old (and) dirty man**

(c) **I think I left a little black book behind**

(d) **I want the little round mirror over there**

(e) **silly old me!**

(f) **you dirty old man, you!**

(g) **this is my cute little sister**

(h) **what an adorable, sweet little cottage!**

In (a-d) **old** and **little** have their literal senses and could, in those senses, easily take up predicative position. But in (e-h) some of the literalness has got lost: **a dirty old man** (= sexual pervert) need not be that old. The reference is more to behaviour than age. **My little sister** in (g) means 'my younger sister'; the person's height is irrelevant. And **little** in (h) is more a description of the speaker's emotion than of the dimensions of the cottage. Similarly in (e), where **old** does not mean 'old' at all.

b) So far we have mentioned only two adjectival positions, **attributive** and **predicative**. There is a third called **appositional**, which is after a noun without a verb intervening. Appositional adjectives (together with any further qualification) are thus similar in function to a relative clause:

this is a custom peculiar to Britain

this is a man confident of success

Adjectives can only be appositional if they can also be predicative, and are particularly common when qualified by a prepositional phrase, as in the examples above. But we also find appositional adjectives used for stylistic emphasis, but only if there is more than one:

her jewellery, cheap and tawdry, was quickly removed

he looked into a face sympathetic but firm

books, new or secondhand, for sale

This position is also relatively common (but by no means obligatory) after the vague words **things** and **matters**:

his long-lasting interest in matters linguistic has finally borne fruit

she has an abhorrence of things English

and for adjectives in **-able** or **-ible**, especially if the noun is preceded by **only** or a superlative:

they committed the worst atrocities imaginable

he's the only person responsible

the only bit visible was the white spot on its paw

c)   Certain adjectives derived from French or Latin are found following their noun in the French manner and in fossilized expressions, eg **poet laureate, the Princess Royal, Lords Spiritual, Lords Temporal, letters patent, lion rampant, devil incarnate**.

4   ADJECTIVES USED AS NOUNS

a)   Adjectives can function as nouns. This usage applies mainly to abstract concepts and to classes or groups of people (either in general or referring to a specific situations):

   i)   Abstract concepts:

   you must take the rough with the smooth

   the use of the symbolic in his films

   ii)   Classes or groups of people:

   we must bury our dead

the poor are poor because they have been oppressed by the rich

And Oscar Wilde's famous description of fox hunters:

the unspeakable in full pursuit of the uneatable

b) An adjective cannot normally replace a singular countable noun. Here **one** is needed (but see further under **one**, p 131):

I don't like the striped shirt; I prefer the plain one

However, there are a few past participles that can be used (with the definite article) to replace a singular countable noun, such as:

the accused (= the accused man or woman)

the deceased/the departed (= the dead man or woman)

the deceased's possessions were sold

Note also **the Almighty** = 'God'.

c) In the plural examples under a) no -s was added to the adjectives, but full conversion from adjective to noun sometimes takes place:

the blacks against the whites in South Africa

the Reds (= the Communists)

here come the newly-weds

please put all the empties in a box (= empty bottles)

he's a drunk

the street was full of drunks

d) *Nationalities*

i) We can distinguish four groups:

(1) pure adjectives
(2) those where the adjective and noun are identical
(3) like (2) except that the noun takes **-s** in the plural
(4) those for which the corresponding noun is a different word (although the plural can be expressed by the noun with **-s**)

Group 1

adjective: **English Literature**

used as a noun (referring to the nation):

the English are rather reserved

Adjectives in Group 1 cannot be used as nouns to refer to individuals. In such cases nouns ending in -**man** (or -**woman**) are used:

we spoke to two Englishmen/Englishwomen

Other examples from Group 1 are **Irish**, **Welsh**, **French**, **Dutch**.

Group 2

adjective: **Japanese art**

used as a noun (referring to the nation):

the Japanese are a hardworking nation

and referring to individuals:

it's hard to interpret the smile of a Japanese
I've got six Japanese in my class

Like **Japanese** are the other words in -**ese**, eg **Chinese**, **Burmese**, **Vietnamese**, **Portuguese**, and also **Swiss**.

Group 3

adjective: **German institutions**

used as a noun (referring to the nation):

the Germans produce some fine cars

and to individuals:

he was having a conversation with a German
we met quite a few Germans on our holiday

Similarly those ending in **-an**, eg:

> **African, American, Asian, Australian, Belgian, Brazilian, Canadian, European, Hungarian, Indian, Iranian, Italian, Norwegian, Russian**

(but note **Arabian** in Group 4 below) and those in **-i**:

> **Iraqi, Israeli, Pakistani.**

Note **Bangladesh** for the adjective (**the Bangladesh economy**), **Bangladeshi** for the person (a **Bangladeshi/three Bangladeshis came to see me**).

Others include **Czech, Cypriot, Greek.**

Group 4

adjective: **Danish furniture**

used as noun (referring to the nation):

> **the Danish know how to eat**

But there is a separate noun form which can also be used to refer to the nation:

> **the Danes know how to eat**

and which is the only form available to refer to individuals:

> **a Dane will always ask you what something costs**

> **there were two Danes in the cast**

Similarly: **British/Briton, Finnish/Finn, Polish/Pole, Spanish/Spaniard, Swedish/Swede.**

Note **Arabian/Arab**: the normal adjective is **Arabian** (**Arabian Nights**) unless we refer to the language or numerals:

the Arabic language is difficult — do you speak Arabic?

thank God for Arabic numerals, I can't cope with the Roman ones

Arab is used for a person unless **Saudi** precedes. Then **Saudi Arabian** or **Saudi** is used:

the hotel has been hired by Saudi Arabians (or **Saudis**)

ii) A note on Scottish, Scots and Scotch:

Nowadays **Scotch** is rare except in fixed combinations (often kinds of food or drink), eg **Scotch egg** (= a large rissole with a whole boiled egg inside), **Scotch whisky**, **Scotch mist** (mist mixed with light rain), **Scotch broth** and **Scotch terrier**.

In cases other than those above, the adjective is normally **Scottish** as in **a Scottish bar**, **Scottish football supporters**, although **Scots** is sometimes used of people: **a Scots lawyer**. Linguists now distinguish between **Scottish English** (= standard English spoken with a Scottish accent) and **Scots** (= the Scottish dialect(s)).

As a noun about the nation **the Scots** (sometimes **the Scottish**) is used. The individual is **a Scot** (plural **Scots**) or **a Scotsman** (plural **Scotsmen**).

5. ADVERBS AND ADVERBIALS

In the following 'adverb' is used for a single word (eg **happily**) and 'adverbial' for a clause or phrase which has an adverbial function.

A. TYPES

1 ADVERBS

a) *Original and derived*

We can distinguish between two kinds of adverbs according to their form: 'original' and 'derived'.

'Derived' means derived from other word classes, for example:

happily	from the adjective **happy**
hourly	from the noun **hour** or the adjective **hourly**
moneywise	from the noun **money**

Examples of 'original' adverbs are:

here	**often**	**now**	**soon**
there	**never**	**then**	**very**

b) *Gradable and non-gradable*

We can also divide adverbs into 'gradable' and 'non-gradable' (see **Adjectives**, p 62). Thus **soon** and **foolishly** are 'gradable':

I wish I could have had this section **sooner**

I'll send you the next section **very soon**

you've acted **extremely foolishly**

whereas, for instance, **now** and **entirely** are 'non-gradable'.

c) *Meaning*

Adverbs can be divided into many types according to meaning. The following are particularly common:

i) Adverbs of time:

now, then, once, soon, always, briefly

I saw her once
you always say that

ii) Adverbs of place:

here, there, everywhere, up, down, back

come here
isn't it time for you to get up?

iii) Adverbs of manner:

well, clumsily, beautifully

if it's worth doing, it's worth doing well
she sang beautifully

iv) Adverbs of degree:

rather, quite, very, hardly, extremely

this gravy is rather good
it was an extremely fine performance

2 ADVERBIAL PHRASES AND CLAUSES

a) *Adverbial phrases*

Apart from adverb phrases (eg **very skilfully**) in which one adverb is used to qualify another, these are mostly prepositional phrases, such as **in a minute**, **after the show**, **to Italy**:

I'll be there in a minute
after the show we can have dinner
he's gone to Italy

but they can also be noun phrases, such as **the hell** and **next week** as used in:

> **I'm not leaving! — the hell you aren't!**
>
> **come and see me next week**

or even (rarely) a single noun:

> **I'm going home**

b) *Adverbial clauses*

Clauses may function adverbially in a sentence. They are recognized by their various conjunctions (see below) and can be divided into the following main types (the adverbial clauses are given outside the brackets in the examples):

i)   Adverbial clauses of time:

> **(don't speak to me) while I'm on the phone**
>
> **as he was driving along(, he saw a field of tulips)**

ii) Adverbial clauses of place:

> **(he always goes) where she goes**
>
> **wherever you are(, I'll find you)**

iii) Adverbial clauses of manner:

> **(do) as I say**
>
> **(he spoke) as if he had a potato in his mouth**
>
> **however hard I try(, I can't do it)**

iv) Adverbial clauses of reason:

> **(do it) because I say so**
>
> **since you've brought it up(, we'd better discuss it)**

v)   Adverbial clauses of concession:

> **(he did it) although he shouldn't have**
>
> **even if he is poor(, he can afford to pay 10p)**

vi) Adverbial clauses of purpose:

(I'll give you a tablet) so that you'll fall asleep

just so that you won't hear anything(, put this cotton wool in your ears)

vii) Adverbial clauses of result:

(the machine never broke down,) so now everything is finished

viii) Adverbial clauses of condition:

(do it) if you dare

unless you tell me(, I can do nothing)

B.   FORMS

a) *Adverbs in -ly*

This ending is normally added directly to the corresponding adjective:

sweet: sweetly

But if the adjective ends in -ic, then -ally is added:

intrinsic: intrinsically

drastic: drastically

The only exceptions are:

public: publicly

and the relatively rare **politic: politicly** (= judicious(ly)).

For spelling changes (as in **happy: happily** or **noble: nobly**) see p 247.

Note that the vowel of -ed is always pronounced in an adverb, whether it is pronounced in the corresponding adjective or not:

assured: assuredly (-e pronounced in adverb only)

offhanded: offhandedly (-e pronounced in both)

b) *Same form as the adjective*

Some adverbs have the same form as their corresponding adjectives, for example:

a fast car

he drives too fast

a hard punch

he hit him hard

And some adverbs can either take the same form as the adjective or add **-ly**:

why are you driving so slow(ly)?

he speaks a bit too quick(ly) for me

The form without **-ly** is sometimes regarded as colloquial English.

For a detailed description of other adverbs in this category see pp 79-91.

c) *Comparison*

Gradable adverbs (see p 71 above) form their comparative and superlative with **-er/-est** or **more/most** in the same way as adjectives.

Adverbs formed by adding -ly to an adjective take **more** and **most**:

these are the most recently published works in this field

But **early**, which has no corresponding adjective without -ly, takes **-er/-est**:

he made himself a promise to get up earlier in future

Adverbs which have the same form as their corresponding adjectives take **-er/-est**:

I can run faster than you think

we arrived earlier than we expected

The adjectives **slow** and **quick** can form adverbs either with **-ly** or without a form change at all (which some consider colloquial) and therefore have two types of comparative:

> **you ought to drive more slowly**
>
> **could you drive a little slower please**
>
> **letters are arriving more quickly than they used to**
>
> **letters are getting through quicker than before**

The following are irregular:

badly	**worse**	**worst**
far	**further, farther**	**furthest, farthest**
little	**less**	**least**
much	**more**	**most**
well	**better**	**best**

The comparative of **late** is **later** (regular); the superlative is **latest** (regular) and **last** (irregular). For the difference in meaning and usage between **latest** and **last** and between **further/furthest** and **farther/farthest**, compare the corresponding adjectives, p 62.

d) *-wise*

The suffix **-wise** may be added to nouns in order to form an adverb which has the general sense of 'as regards (whatever the noun may be)':

> **how's he feeling? — do you mean mentally or healthwise?**

Although quite common, this construction tends to be more spoken than written English, and is not always regarded as particularly good style, especially in the more 'creative' uses:

> **things are going quite well schedule-wise**
>
> **we're not really short of anything furniture-wise**
>
> **the town's quite well provided restaurant-wise**

C. USE

1 ADVERBIAL FUNCTIONS

Adverbs and adverbials are used to modify

(1) verbs:

> **he spoke well**
> **he spoke in a loud voice**

(2) adjectives:

> **that's awfully nice of you**
> **this isn't good enough**

(3) other adverbs:

> **she didn't sing very well**
> **she didn't sing well enough**
> **it happened extremely quickly**

(Note that **enough** follows the adjective or adverb that it modifies)

(4) nouns which are used predicatively like adjectives:

> **this is rather a mess** (= this is rather messy)
> **he's quite a hero**

(5) (pro)nouns, when the adverbial is used in a semi-predicative manner (ie normally after a form of **be**):

> **the manager is in**
> **the meeting will be tomorrow**
> **this one is for you**

(6) the whole sentence:

> **fortunately they accepted the verdict**
> **this is obviously a problem**
> **amazingly enough, it was true**

2 ADVERBS WITH ADJECTIVAL FORMS

a) *Adverb and adjective always identical*

These include eg:

**far, fast
little, long
early, only**

and quite a few in **-ly** derived from nouns (often referring to time), eg:

**daily, monthly
weekly, deathly, leisurely**

he travelled to far and distant lands (adjective)
he travelled far and wide (adverb)

this is a fast train (adjective)
you're driving too fast (adverb)

he bought a little house (adjective)
little do you care! (adverb)

Churchill loved those long cigars (adjective)
have you been here long? (adverb)

you'll have to catch the early plane (adjective)
they arrived early (adverb)

she's an only child (adjective)
I've only got 10p (adverb)

do you get a daily newspaper? (adjective)
there's a flight twice daily (adverb)

you'll receive this in monthly instalments (adjective)
the list will be updated monthly (adverb)

a deathly silence fell on the spectators (adjective)
she was deathly pale (adverb)

we took a leisurely stroll after dinner (adjective)

his favourite pastime is travelling leisurely along the
Californian coast (adverb)

b) *Adverb and adjective sometimes identical*

Certain adverbs sometimes have -ly, sometimes not, and
there is often a difference in meaning between the two
forms. The following are particularly interesting:

★ **clean/cleanly**

Clean is an adverb of degree = 'completely, all the
way':

we're clean out of toilet paper (colloquial)

the arrow went clean through his heart

I clean forgot (colloquial)

Cleanly is used in the various senses of the adjective:

he lives cleanly and soberly, almost like a monk

luckily the bone had broken cleanly

★ **clear/clearly**

Like **clean**, **clear** is an adverb of degree:

the escapees had got clear away

In the senses of the adjective, **clearly** is normally used:

you have clearly forgotten your duties

but it is possible to say:

speak loud and clear

★ **close/closely**

Close emphasizes degree, **closely** emphasizes manner:

hold me close!

they followed close behind

study it closely

he followed her closely with his eyes

★   **dead/deadly**

Both are adverbs of degree, but **dead** has lost all association with **death**. **Deadly** has not in many cases, and even when it gets close to **dead** in meaning, it remains more descriptive:

I'm dead certain (colloquial)

the dogs are dead tired

go dead slow here

her face became deadly pale

he's deadly slow

this is deadly dull

★   **dear/dearly**

In the literal sense 'at a high price' **dear** is normal (compare **cheap** above):

buy cheap and sell dear

In the figurative sense both forms are possible, though **dearly** is normal before the verb:

this will cost you dear

he paid dearly for his indiscretion

his was a dearly bought victory

★   **deep/deeply**

Deeply is normally used in a figurative sense only:

they are deeply in love

he was deeply offended by her remark

Deep is literal or figurative, but not as figurative as **deeply**, which often means 'profoundly' (**deep** cannot be used in this way):

to find the body you'll have to dig deeper

deep inside he felt deeply hurt

★ **direct/directly**

Both are used with reference to direction (= straight), **direct** being particularly common with **go**, **come**, **fly**, **send**:

you can now fly from Aberdeen to Denmark direct

send it direct(ly) to me

Directly often emphasizes the manner:

she looked directly at him

This is why **directly** is preferred in the figurative sense:

she answered him directly

this has directly affected our sales

Directly is also used with reference to time (= very soon):

she will be here directly

★ **due/duly**

Due with the four points of the compass, otherwise **duly**:

they went due east (= straight)

the letter you posted yesterday has duly arrived

they were duly appointed co-directors

★ **easy/easily**

Easy is always used in:

take it/things easy

easy come, easy go

easy does it! (= do it gently)

go easy on somebody (= treat somebody more gently)

and in the military command:

stand easy!

Easier said than done is also heard much more often than **more easily said than done**.

When the meaning is clearly 'without difficulty' or 'without doubt', then **easily** is used:

I can easily finish it by Monday

he is easily the best qualified candidate

★   **fair/fairly**

Both can be used with the same meaning as the adjective, but **fair** is normally confined to set combinations, especially: **play/fight fair** and **fair and square**:

come on now, play fair!

he's treated everyone fair and square

please judge us fairly

they don't play the game fairly

Both forms can also be used as adverbs of degree. **Fair** is used in the sense 'directly' and in **bid fair**:

I hit him fair on the chin (dialect, colloquial)

the journey bids fair to be a pleasant one (= seems likely, literary usage)

As an adverb of degree **fairly** means either 'for the most part' or 'completely':

this is fairly accurate (for the most part)

I was fairly taken aback (completely)

★   **false/falsely**

False only in **play (somebody) false**, which means 'to deceive somebody', normally in love affairs:

she played him false

Otherwise **falsely**:

they spoke and acted falsely

★ **first/firstly**

> In the sense 'in the first place' both are used:

> **First(ly) I'd like to point out that this is impossible;
> second(ly) even if it weren't, we couldn't afford it;
> third(ly) . . .**

> The other ordinal adverbs (**second(ly)**, **third(ly)** etc and
> **last(ly)**) are less likely to omit **-ly** than is **first(ly)** —
> except in the set expression **last but not least**.

> In other adverbial senses only **first** is used:

> **first wash up, then you can go to the disco**

> **do you remember when we first met?**

★ **flat/flatly**

> In the sense of 'firmly, directly' both forms occur after
> the verb:

> **she told him flat(ly) that he'd have to leave**

> Before the verb only **flatly** is used:

> **she flatly refused to leave**

> If the meaning is 'in a dull manner', only **flatly** is used:

> **are you asking me to leave yet again?, he asked flatly**

> Note the colloquial uses of **flat out** meaning 'at top
> speed' or 'exhausted':

> **I've been working flat out for the last three weeks**

> **after the party she was flat out**

> In the musical sense 'under the note' (as opposed to
> **sharp**) only **flat** is used:

> **even Callas would sometimes sing flat**

★ **free/freely**

> **Free** = 'without paying, costing nothing' or 'without
> restriction on one's liberty'.

> **Freely** = 'openly; without hindrance':

here, where the lions can wander free

I freely admit that I made a mistake

There is a considerable difference between saying:

dogs travel free on buses
and
dogs travel freely on buses

★   full/fully

Full = 'directly, straight':

she looked him full in the face

Note also full well, full out:

you know full well that it isn't true (= very well)

he was riding his bike full out round the corner

Otherwise fully is used:

we're fully booked
we fully understand your problem
he explained fully and clearly the difficulties of the task

★   hard/hardly

In the sense of 'with great effort or force' hard is used:

work hard!

he took it hard (= suffered greatly)

it's raining quite hard

prejudices die hard

you have to blow harder

Hardly means 'almost not', a very common sense
(which hard does not share):

I hardly know her

you've hardly touched your food

hardly had I started my meal when the phone rang

Note the word order inversion in the last example when
hardly comes at the beginning of a sentence.

★ **high/highly**

Highly is used in a figurative sense as an adverb of degree meaning 'extremely' or 'very':

your call was highly appreciated

she is highly efficient

I should think that's highly unlikely

High is used in a literal sense:

we're flying high above the sea

or in certain fixed figurative senses:

emotions ran high

★ **just/justly**

If the meaning is that of the adjective, then **justly** is used:

he was justly accused

Otherwise **just**:

this is just right (= exactly)

I've just finished my dinner (= a moment ago)

just two for me thanks (= only)

★ **large/largely**

Large is used only in **by and large** (= mainly):

it is not always true, but by and large it is

Largely has the same sense:

this is largely true (= mainly)

it's largely a matter of personal preference

★ **late/lately**

Late is the opposite of **early**:

they arrived late

Lately means 'recently':

he hasn't been well lately

* **loud/loudly/aloud**

   In the literal sense both **loud** and **loudly** are used.
   Loud tends to be confined to common verbs like **speak,
   talk, laugh, sing, play**, which can also be found with
   loudly in certain cases:

   don't play any louder; we can't hear the singers

   don't talk so loud!

   they were talking loudly amongst themselves

   they protested loudly

   Figuratively only **loudly** is used:

   he was loudly dressed (= too colourfully)

   Aloud normally means 'in an audible voice':

   would you read it aloud to me?

* **low/lowly**

   Low is used in the various literal senses of the
   adjective:

   aim low and you might hit it

   he was sitting at the desk, bent low over his books

   **he bowed low and remained in that position for at
   least a minute**

   I can't sing that low

   supplies are running low

   Lowly is used in figurative senses (in which a different
   construction with **low** would also be possible):

   these men are among the lowly paid workers

   these men are among the low-paid workers

* **most/mostly**

   When the meaning is 'mainly', then **mostly** is used,
   otherwise **most**:

   the things you see there are mostly rubbish

the answers were mostly correct

a husband is what she needs most of all

the money rarely goes to those most in need of it

★ **near/nearly**

Near is used in the sense of 'not far':

do you live near?

Note, however, the figurative sense of **near** in the construction **nowhere near**:

that's nowhere near enough

it's half past and we're still nowhere near ready!

Nearly is used in the sense of 'almost':

I nearly forgot your birthday

Note that the negative construction **not nearly** is used in the sense of 'by no means':

that's not nearly enough

★ **quick/quickly**

The two are often used interchangeably although **quick** is particularly frequent in colloquial speech:

come quick — the ice-cream van's here!

he walked back to his house quickly and determinedly

Before a verb **quickly** is used:

he quickly came to his senses

unless a compound is formed as in **quick-thinking, quick-witted**.

The comparative and superlative are often **quicker** and **quickest** even when the corresponding absolute would normally be **quickly**:

he answered quickly

you'll have to answer quicker than that

he answered quickest of them all

* **right/rightly**

    In the sense of 'correctly', 'properly', 'justly', both can be used, but only **rightly** is used before the verb:

    if I remember right(ly), it has been posted

    serves you right! (not **rightly**)

    did I do it right (not **rightly**)

    she doesn't treat him right (not **rightly**)

    they sacked him, and rightly so (not **right**)

    you've been rightly informed

    she is rightly considered one of the great sopranos of our time

    Only **right** is used before other adverbials in the sense of 'straight' or 'exactly':

    go right in

    he put it right in front of the telly

    I want you to come right now

    and, of course, as the opposite of 'left' as in:

    turn right at the next corner

* **rough/roughly**

    Rough is confined to a few set combinations:

    they have been living/sleeping rough for a while (= in rough conditions, especially out of doors)

    they certainly play (it) rough (= use a good deal of force)

    he cut up rough (= got angry)

    Otherwise normally **roughly** is used:

    he has been roughly treated

    he treated her rough(ly)

    In the sense of 'about' only **roughly** is used:

    we can get roughly 60 people in here

★ sharp/sharply

Both are used in the sense 'at an acute angle', 'suddenly' or 'quickly':

there is a small café just where the road turns sharp(ly) to the right

they turned sharp(ly) around

turn sharp left by the church (not **sharply**)

Sharp is always used in **look sharp** and **pull up sharp**:

look sharp or you'll miss your bus (= hurry, colloquial)

you'd better look sharp when he's around (= watch out, colloquial)

the car pulled up sharp (= came to a sudden halt)

In the musical sense only **sharp** is used:

the brass section is playing a little sharp again

★ short/shortly

Short can be used in the sense of 'suddenly', especially after **stop** and **pull up**:

he stopped short to avoid hitting the cat

she pulled her horse up short just before getting to the fence

Short is also used in many idioms, eg **cut short** 'stop (somebody or something) before the end', **fall short (of)** 'not be good enough (for)', **go short (of)** 'be without', **run short** (compare **run low** under **low**) 'become insufficient':

she cut him short in the middle of his story

this fell short of our expectations

here's a fiver; I don't want you to go short

our supplies are running short

we're running short of money

Shortly is used to mean 'briefly' or 'soon':

he should be here shortly

shortly after this the tide of events turned

Shortly is also used to mean 'in a short manner' or 'curtly':

I think not, she said shortly

★ **slow/slowly**

For the literal sense **slow** is common in colloquial English. **Slowly** is often more descriptive:

drive slow! (eg on signposts)

go dead slow here

he drove slowly round the corner

he rose and came slowly towards her

★ **sound/soundly**

Sound is normally confined to the phrase **sound asleep**:

the children are sound asleep in bed

Otherwise use **soundly**:

she sleeps soundly these days

a soundly argued case

★ **thick/thickly**

Thick is an adverb of degree, which becomes **thickly** before the verb:

they are thick on the ground (= there are lots of them)

the snow lay thick on the hills

he smeared the substance thick on the wall

the blows fell thick and fast

all the bread was thickly covered in mould

As an adverb of manner only **thickly** is used:

he spoke thickly and with some difficulty

* **tight/tightly**

In many cases there is little difference in meaning:

he held her tightly in his arms

hold me tight!

pull the curtains tight

have I fastened it too tight(ly)?

this lid doesn't close tight(ly)

he closed the lid tight(ly)

But **tightly** is used before a past participle:

it was hard to remove the tightly closed lid

And in certain set expressions only **tight** is used:

good night, sleep tight

the hall was packed tight for the concert

* **wrong/wrongly**

Wrong is obligatory in **go wrong** and **get something wrong**:

from that moment things started to go wrong

you've got it all wrong

you've got your sums wrong

Following the object (as in the last two examples) **wrong** is frequent in many other instances although **wrongly** is also used:

you've spelt the word wrong(ly)

he did his sums wrong(ly)

Only **wrongly** can be used before the verb:

he was wrongly accused of the theft

they wrongly maintained that ...

look at these wrongly spelt words

these sums have been wrongly added up

3 POSITION OF THE ADVERB

a) *Adverbs of time*

i) If these refer to a definite time, they are normally positioned at the end of the sentence:

the shops close at 8 tonight

will I see you tomorrow?

Positioning an adverb at the beginning of a sentence can lend more weight:

tomorrow it'll be too late

But the little word **now** often precedes the verb:

I now see the point

now I see the point

I see the point now

ii) If the reference is to indefinite time, the normal position is before the main verb:

I always buy my shirts here

we soon got to know him

we have often talked about it

they have frequently discussed such matters

they are rarely seen to smoke

But such adverbs normally follow forms of **be**:

he's never late

they are rarely here

he was frequently in trouble with the police

If there is more than one auxiliary, these adverbs tend to precede the second, but may, for emphasis, follow it:

she has frequently been visited by distant relatives

she has been frequently visited ...

b) *Adverbs of place*

These follow the verb (and object):

> **they travelled everywhere**
> **they have gone back**
> **I saw you there**
> **we have often stayed here**

but note frequent initial position before **be**:

> **there's the postman**
> **here are your books**

and before personal pronouns used with **be, come** and **go**:

> **there he is**
> **here she comes**
> **there they go**

c) *Adverbs of manner*

  i) Very often the position of an adverb will make no difference to the basic meaning of a sentence, there being considerable flexibility here in English with a lot of scope for the writer's or speaker's intentions as regards overtones, nuances and sentence pattern:

> **they stealthily crept upstairs**
> **they crept stealthily upstairs**
> **they crept upstairs stealthily**
> **stealthily, they crept upstairs**
> **she carefully examined the report**
> **she examined the report carefully**
> **it was beautifully done**
> **it was done beautifully**

But, in some cases, if the writer or speaker of a sentence wants to stress the adverb, the strongest position is at the end of a sentence. Compare, for example:

they ran quickly upstairs

they ran upstairs quickly

The more the manner is emphasized the more likely the adverb is to follow the verb.

In the following only one position is possible:

they fought the war intelligently

ii) If the object is of considerable length, end position is normally avoided:

she carefully examined the report sent to her by the Minister

iii) Initial position is very descriptive or emphatic:

clumsily he made his way towards the door

iv) Adverbs modifying sentences/adverbs modifying verbs:

Compare the following:

(a) **she spoke wisely at the meeting**

(b) **she wisely spoke at the meeting**

In (a) **wisely** is a clear adverb of manner. In (b) it is not an adverb of manner at all; it does not describe the manner of speaking. Instead it comments on the whole sentence and means 'it was a wise thing for her to speak at the meeting'. Some other examples:

she spoke naturally and fluently (modifying verb)

she naturally assumed it was right (modifying sentence)

naturally she assumed it was right (modifying sentence)

she accepted the invitation happily (modifying verb)

she happily accepted the invitation (modifying verb)

happily she accepted the invitation (modifying sentence = fortunately)

she understood it clearly (modifying verb)

she clearly understood it (modifying sentence or verb)

clearly she understood it (modifying sentence)

The word **enough** can also be used after an adverb to make it clear that the adverb is being used in a sentence-modifying way:

funnily (enough), they both spoke at the meeting

d) *Adverbs of degree*

  i) If these modify adverbs, adjectives or nouns, they precede those words:

  she played extremely well

  this is very good

  it's too hot to eat

  it's rather a mess

  ii) Otherwise they normally precede the main verb:

  I nearly forgot your anniversary

  I could hardly remember a thing

  I merely asked

  we just want to know the time of departure

  we very much enjoyed your book

  they also prefer white wine

  But **too** (in the sense of 'also') normally follows what it modifies:

  you too should go and see the exhibition

  you should try to see that exhibition too

iii) **only**

This adverb rarely poses any difficulties in spoken English because stress and intonation reveal the meaning:

(a) **Bill only *saw* Bob today** (= but didn't speak to him)

(b) **Bill only saw *Bob* today** (= he saw nobody else)

(c) **Bill only saw Bob *today*** (= he saw him today only/he didn't see him before today)

Such differences are obscured in written language unless the context is clear. Thus (b) in written language would probably be changed to:

Bill saw only Bob today

and (c) to:

it was only today that Bill saw Bob

In (a) italics would probably be used:

Bill only *saw* Bob today

iv) **very** or **much**?

★ Before adjectives in the absolute **very** is used:

these are very fine

also before the superlative in -est:

these are the very finest copies I've seen
my very dearest Joanna!

In the following alternative superlative construction, however, **much** is used before the 'the' of the superlative:

this is much the best example in the book
she is much the most intelligent person here

★ The comparative has **much**:

she's much taller than you
she's much more particular

★ Similarly with adverbs:

you do it very well, but I do it much better

★ Verbs take **much** (which itself is modified by **very**):

I love you very much

★ Before past participles:

If these function like adjectives, then **very** is used; but if they retain their verbal force (often indicated by the 'doer' in a following **by**-phrase), then **much** is preferred:

I'm very tired

he is very well-spoken

we've become very interested in this house

they became very offended

they sat there, all very agitated

I'm very pleased to meet you

these suitcases are looking very used

this has been much spoken about (not 'very')

these suitcases haven't been much used (not 'very')

he has been much maligned (not 'very')

they were much taken aback by the reception they received (also 'very')

his new house is much admired by people round here (not 'very')

In colloquial language **a lot** is often preferred to **much**:

these haven't been used a lot

v) **enough:**

As an adverb **enough** comes after the adjective:

he isn't big enough for that yet

It also comes after a noun used predicatively like an adjective:

he isn't man enough for the job

Note that **enough** may separate adjective and noun:

he's a decent enough fellow

e)   *Adverbs modifying the whole sentence*

These are very flexible as regards position; see further the discussion under **Adverbs of manner** above, p 94. Here are some examples of sentences modified by adverbs which are not used as adverbs of manner:

probably that isn't true
that probably isn't true
fortunately he stopped in time
he fortunately stopped in time
he stopped in time, fortunately
really, I don't think so
I really don't think so
I don't think so, really

f)   *Position of not*

i)   **Not** precedes the adverbial it modifies:

is he here? − not yet
do you mind? − not at all
he speaks not only English, but also French
he lives not far from here

In the following example it is **absolutely** that qualifies **not**, not vice versa:

have you said something to her? − absolutely not

ii)   **Not** follows **be**:

he is not hungry

iii) Since **do** is used when a main verb is negated, there is always at least one auxiliary in such cases. **Not** (or **-n't**) normally follows the first auxiliary:

he does not smoke/he doesn't smoke

they have not seen her/they haven't seen her

But in questions the full **not** follows the subject, whereas **n't** precedes it, being tied to the auxiliary:

did they not shout abuse at her?

didn't they shout abuse at her?

have they not shouted abuse at her?

haven't they shouted abuse at her?

iv) In American English **not** may precede a subjunctive:

it is important that he not be informed of this

v) Note also the following:

did you do it? − not me

vi) Note the type seen in:

will she come? − I hope not

Here **not** negates **will come** (I hope she won't come)

6. PRONOUNS

A. TYPES

personal (*eg* **you, he**)
reflexive (*eg* **myself, ourselves**)
possessive (*eg* **your(s), their(s)**)
demonstrative (*eg* **that, these**)
interrogative (*eg* **who, which, what**)
relative (**who, which, that, what**)
indefinite (*eg* **some(body), any(thing), each, (n)either**)

B. FORMS

PERSONAL

	singular	*plural*
1st	**I/me**	**we/us**
2nd	**you**	**you**
3rd	**he/him, she/her, it**	**they/them**

REFLEXIVE

	singular	*plural*
1st	**myself**	**ourselves**
2nd	**yourself**	**yourselves**
3rd	**himself, herself itself, oneself**	**themselves**

POSSESSIVE

	singular	*plural*
1st	**my/mine**	**our/ours**
2nd	**your/yours**	**your/yours**
3rd	**his, her/hers, its**	**their/theirs**

DEMONSTRATIVE

singular	*plural*
this, that	**these, those**

INTERROGATIVE

who/whom/whose, **which**, **what** and combinations with
-ever, eg **whichever**

RELATIVE

who/whom/whose, **which**, **what**, **that** and
combinations with **-ever**, eg **whichever**

INDEFINITE

some(body), **someone**, **something**
any(body), **anyone**, **anything**
no(body), **no one**, **none**, **nothing**
every(body), **(an)other**, **others**
either, **neither**, **both**, **one**
every(body), **everyone**, **everything**
each, **all**, **(an)other**, **others**, **either**, **both**, **one**

Note that those in **-body** and **-one** can have genitive forms, eg
anybody's, **someone's**. So can **one**, **(an)other**, **either**, **neither**,
eg **one's**, **another's**.

C. USE

1 PERSONAL PRONOUNS

a) *Subject form or object form*

i) Normally the subject forms (**I, you, he, she, we, they**)
    are used for the subject. Examples like:

me and the wife are always there

are incorrect though commonly heard. But English
often uses the object forms (**me, him, her, us, them**) in
instances where many languages use the subject forms:

who is it? − it's me

let Henry go and speak to her − what? him?

who did it? − me (or I did)

It is I/he/she etc would be considered almost comically
formal.

However, if a relative clause follows, the subject forms are not infrequent provided the relative pronoun functions as subject:

it was I who did it

it was me that did it (colloquial)

but always:

it was me (that) you spoke to

The subject form **I** is frequent in the phrase **between you and I**. This hypercorrect usage is frowned on by some, who prefer **between you and me**. See further under **Reflexive Pronouns**, p 109.

ii) After **than** and **as** we normally hear the object form (if no verb follows):

she's not as good as him, but better than me

but (with a verb):

she's not as good as he is, but better than I am

However, the subject forms can be in the final position after **than** and **as** in more formal language, especially after **than**:

he is a better man than I

b) *Omission of the subject pronoun*

As opposed to a number of other European languages, English does not omit the subject pronoun — though, as with nearly everything, there are exceptions:

i) Omission of **it**:

in informal language the third person singular pronoun **it** may be omitted in contexts like:

looks like rain this afternoon

what do you think of it? — sounds/smells good

But this is not a feature that can be freely applied to any sentence.

ii) Special effects:

Pronouns can be omitted when a list of verbs follows a subject:

I know the place well, go there once a week, even thought about moving there

iii) Imperatives:

Of course, with the imperative, subject pronouns are standardly omitted:

don't do that!

and are included only for special emphasis (eg a threatening tone):

don't you do that!

c) *he, she or it?*

He (**him**, **his**) or **she** (**her**) are sometimes used about non-persons, ie animals and certain things, but only if the speaker has a relatively intimate relation to, or shows great personal interest in, the animal or object. If not, **it** is used.

i) Animals:

Fluffy is getting on: she probably won't give birth to any more kittens

they simply couldn't bring themselves to send her to the slaughterhouse, so she was allowed to stay in the field in peace

the poor old dog, take him for a walk, can't you!

but:

a dog's senses are very keen; it can hear much higher frequencies than we can

ii) Means of transport:

Normally the feminine **she** is used, unless there is a special reason (which can be purely personal):

she's been a long way, this old car

there she is! – the 'Titanic' in all her glory! (about ship)

but:

**this ship is larger than that one, and it has an extra
funnel**

**the 'Flying Scotsman' will soon have made his/her last
journey** (about train)

iii) Countries:

**and Denmark? – she will remember those who died
for her**

but:

**Denmark is a small country; it is almost surrounded by
water**

d) *it without reference*

i) In contrast to many other languages English often uses
it as a subject although the subject does not point to
anything specific. This is the case in statements about
the weather, in evaluations and when describing
situations:

it's raining

it's freezing in here

what's it like outside today?

it's very cosy here

it's wrong to steal

it's not easy to raise that sort of money

it's clear they don't like it

it looks as if/seems/appears that they've left

Also in references to points in time and distance:

it's ten o'clock

it's June the tenth

it's time to go

it's at least three miles

But if the reference is to length of time, **there** is used:

there's still time to mend matters

Note also the phrase **it says** when referring to a text:

it says in today's 'Times' that a hurricane is on its way

ii) As subject complement or object, **it** can also be used non-referentially, especially in fixed phrases:

this is it! (= the important point or moment)

she thinks she's it (= she thinks she's important or very attractive, colloquial)

the bull seals were lording it over harems of up to twenty females (= behaving like great masters)

beat it! (= go away, colloquial)

she has it in for him (= she treats him badly, colloquial)

have they had it off? (= have they had sex?, colloquial)

e) *Generic Usage*

You, **we** and **they** are often used generically in the sense 'people in general'. The difference between them is essentially that if **you** is used, the person spoken to is normally included in the 'people', whereas if the speaker uses **we** he emphasizes his own inclusion. **They** refers to other people in general:

you don't see many prostitutes in Aberdeen any more

I'm afraid we simply don't treat animals very well

they say he beats his wife

i) **You** used to comment on a situation:

you never can find one when you need one

you never can be too careful

ii) **You** used when giving instructions:

you first crack the eggs into a bowl

you must look both ways before crossing

See also **one** on p 107.

f) *Special uses of we*

Apart from the generic use (see p 105), two more should be mentioned:

i) the royal **we** (= **I**), as in Queen Victoria's famous remark:

we are not amused

ii) the patronizing or humorous **we** (= **you**), particularly common among nurses or teachers:

and how are we today, Mr Jenkins?, could we eat just a teeny-weeny portion of porridge?

I see, Smith, forgotten our French homework, have we?

g) *Use of they*

i) The use of generic **they** has become very common with reference to the indefinite pronouns **somebody**, **someone**, **anybody**, **anyone**, **everybody**, **everyone**, **nobody**, **no one**. Generic **they** avoids the clumsy **he** or **she** (sometimes written **s/he**).

He on its own referring to people in general is now considered inappropriate by quite a few people. Generic **they (their, them(selves))** is now normal in spoken (and much written) English (even if only one sex is being referred to) and offers a convenient way of avoiding references which may otherwise be considered sexist:

if anybody has anything against it, they should say so

everybody grabbed their few possessions and ran

somebody has left their bike right outside

This usage is now becoming very common with nouns preceded not only by **any**, **some** or **no** but also by the generic indefinite article:

some person or other has tampered with my files — they'll be sorry

> no child is allowed to leave until they have been seen by a doctor
>
> a person who refuses to use a deodorant may find themselves quietly shunned at parties etc

For the use of **one**, see below.

ii) **They** is used to refer to an unknown person or unknown people who have power, authority or expertise:

> they will have to arrest the entire pit
>
> they should be able to repair it
>
> they will be able to tell you at the advice centre
>
> when you earn a bit of money they always find a way of taking it off you

This use has given rise to the expression 'them and us' which is used to describe those who have the power (them) and those who have not (us).

h) *Generic one*

One is used as subject and as object. The possessive form is **one's**.

i) When **one** is generic the speaker includes himself amongst 'people in general':

> well what can one do?
>
> one is not supposed to do that

One can be useful to avoid possible misinterpretation of the (commmon) use of **you** as in:

> you need to express yourself more clearly

If the speaker is speaking about what a person generally needs to do as opposed to what a particular person needs to do, then this sentence could be clarified as:

> one needs to express oneself more clearly

However, excessive or repetitive use of this pronoun is usually avoided.

ii) Use of **one** with first person reference, ie as a substitute for **I** (or **we**), is now considered rather precious (in the sense of 'too refined' or 'too genteel'):

> **seeing such misery has taught one to appreciate how lucky one is in one's own country**

> **one doesn't like to be deprived of one's little pleasures, does one?**

In American English third person (masculine) pronouns can refer back to generic **one**:

> **one shouldn't take risks if he can avoid it**

i) *it or so?*

Compare:

(a)   **she managed to escape — I can quite believe it**

(b)   **did she manage to escape? — I believe so**

The 'believing' is stronger in (a) where it is close to 'being convinced'. In (b) **believe** is more vague and is synonymous with 'think'. Similarly **it** is a precise object, **so** a less precise adverb of manner. Some other examples of **it/so** referring to a previous statement:

> **it's a difficult job, but I can do it**

> **you promised to call me but didn't (do so)**

> **you're a common thief! there, I've said it**

> **you're a common thief! — if you say so**

Other verbs that frequently take **so** include **expect, hope, seem, suppose, tell**:

> **has he left? — it seems so**

> **I knew it would happen, I told you so**

2 REFLEXIVE PRONOUNS

a) Used as subject complement, direct object, indirect object, and after prepositions to refer to the subject:

I am not myself today (subject complement)

she has burnt herself (direct object)

every weekend we give ourselves a treat (indirect object)

why are you talking to yourself? (after preposition)

But in references to space or direction (literal or figurative) the personal pronouns are often preferred after prepositions:

we have a long day in front of us

she put her bag beside her

have you got any cash on you?

she married beneath her

he has his whole life before him

but always **beside + -self** in the figurative sense:

they were beside themselves with worry

b) *Emphatic use*

If the speaker wishes to emphasize the person/thing referred to then a reflexive pronoun is often used, as in:

you're quite well-off now, aren't you? − you haven't done so badly yourself

only they themselves know whether it is the right thing

get me a beer, will you? − get it yourself

for the work to be done properly, one has to do it oneself

The position of the reflexive can affect meaning:

the PM (Prime Minister) wanted to speak to him herself (ie she wanted to speak to him in person)

but

the PM herself wanted to speak to him (it was none other than the PM who wanted to speak to him)

c) *After as, like, than and and*

After these words many people frequently use the reflexive pronouns rather than the personal ones, sometimes perhaps because they are sensitive to the occasionally awkward choice between subject form and object form (see **Personal Pronouns** above, 1a):

he's not quite as old as myself

like yourself I also have a few family problems

this job needs people more experienced than ourselves

he said it was reserved specially for you and myself

d) *Reflexive verbs*

i) Some (not many) verbs can be reflexive only, eg **absent oneself, avail oneself, betake oneself, demean oneself, ingratiate oneself, perjure oneself, pride oneself.**

ii) Others have totally different meanings depending on whether they are reflexive or not:

he applied for the post

he applied himself to the matter in hand

iii) And there are quite a few verbs whose meaning remains the same with or without the reflexive pronoun:

they always behave (themselves) in public

we found it very difficult to adjust (ourselves) to the humid climate

although the reflexive element may add a sense of determination.

Compare:

(a) **he proved to be useful** (= turned out to be useful)

(b) **so as not to face redundancy, he'll have to prove himself more useful** (= show that he's more useful)

(c) **the crowd pushed forward**

(d) **the crowd pushed itself forward**

In (d) there is more determination than in (c).

3 POSSESSIVE PRONOUNS

a) *Bound or free*

The forms **mine, yours, hers, ours, theirs** are used only as 'free' possessives, ie without a following noun. **My**, **your**, **her**, **our**, **their** are 'bound' to a noun (and are sometimes also called 'possessive adjectives'), and **his**, **its** are both bound and free:

> **this is my hat/this hat is mine**
>
> **her new bag has gone/I prefer hers**

Note the 'double genitive' (compare p 53):

> **he's an old friend of mine**
>
> **that mother of hers is driving me mad**

Note also **Yours (sincerely, faithfully)** followed by the writer's name at the end of a letter.

b) *Possessive or article*

English sometimes uses a possessive pronoun where other languages prefer the definite article. This is often the case in reference to parts of the body or to clothes:

> **he put his hands behind his back**
>
> **she covered her face with her hands**
>
> **he moved his foot an inch or two**
>
> **he pulled his hat over his ears**
>
> **what have you got in your pockets?**

but in a prepositional phrase, the definite article is normally used (although both are possible):

> **he grabbed her by the waist**
>
> **he was hit on the mouth**

But if that part-of-the-body word is itself qualified by an adjective then the possessive and not the article is used:

> **he grabbed her by her slim little waist**

See also **the distributive plural** under **Nouns**, p 48.

4 DEMONSTRATIVE PRONOUNS

a) **This** and **these** refer to something **close** to the speaker or of **immediate** relevance to him, whereas **that** and **those** have a more distant reference. **This/these** are to **here/now** what **that/those** are to **there/then**:

    (a)   **this red pen is mine; that one is yours**

    (b)   **that red pen is mine; this one is yours**

In (a) the red pen is closer to the speaker than the other pen; in (b) it is the other way round.

Other examples:

> **I want to go − you can't mean that**

> **this is what I want you to do: take the baby to Annette's, collect the washing, and telephone the travel agency**

> **this is Christine, is that Joanna?** (on the telephone)

When 'free' (see **Possessives** p 111) the demonstratives cannot refer to persons unless they are the subject or subject complement:

> **this is Carla**

> **who is this?**

Thus in:

> **would you take this?**

this cannot be a person.

b) *Indefinite this/these*

The use of **this/these** as indefinite pronouns is very common in colloquial spoken English at the beginning of a story, often a joke:

> **this Irishman was sitting in a pub when . . .**

> **the other day these guys came up to me . . .**

In such examples **this** = 'a (certain)' and **these** = 'some', 'a couple of'.

c) *Adverbial that/this*

In spoken English **that/this** are often used adverbially, roughly like **so**, before an adjective or other adverb:

> I like a red carpet but not one that red

> I'll do it again, but I really don't like doing it that/this often

> now that we've come this far, we can just as well press on

> I don't want that/this much to eat!

> she doesn't want to support him, she's not that liberated

5 INTERROGATIVE PRONOUNS

a) *who and whom*

Who and **whom** are always free pronouns (ie a noun cannot follow) and refer to persons:

> who are you?

> to whom did you address your remarks?

Whom is used only in formal language, where it functions as object (direct or indirect) or prepositional complement:

> whom did she embrace?

> to whom did he give his permission?

> I demanded to know to whom he had spoken

or

> I demanded to know whom he had spoken to

In everyday spoken English **who** is normally used in all functions. (**Whom** is obligatory directly **after** a preposition, but such a construction is not everyday spoken English.) Examples:

> who did you see at the party?

> I want to know who you spoke to just now

> I want to know to whom you spoke just now (more formal)

b) *whose*

This is the genitive of **who**. It can be free as well as bound:

> **whose are these bags?**
>
> **whose bags are these?**

c) *which/what*

In contrast to **who(m)**, **which** can be both bound and free and refer to both persons and non-persons:

> **which actor do you mean?**
>
> **which of the actors do you mean?**
>
> **of these two recordings, which do you prefer?**
>
> **which of these two recordings do you prefer?**

The difference between **which** and **who/what** is that **which** is limiting; it invites the listener to choose from a restricted number. Compare:

> **what would you like to drink?**
>
> **I've got coffee or tea — which would you like?**

The restriction must be clear, explicitly or implicitly. If it is added as an afterthought or as further clarification, **which** is not used. Compare:

> **which do you prefer? — the red one or the green one?**

but:

> **what would you like to drink? — I've got sherry or vermouth or Campari**

d) *what*

When free, **what** is non-personal only:

> **what is this object?**
>
> **don't ask me what I did**

except that it can refer to personal characteristics:

> **what is he like? — oh, very nice, really**

When bound, **what** can refer to both person and non-person:

> **what child does not like sweets?**
>
> **what kind of powder do you use?**

For the difference between **what** and **which**, see c) above.

Note the use of **what** in exclamations:

> **what awful weather!**
>
> **what a dreadful day!**
>
> **what must they think!**

e) *With -ever*

The universalizing suffix **-ever** expresses surprise, confusion or annoyance:

> **whatever do you mean?** (confusion or annoyance)
>
> **whoever would have thought of that?** (surprise)
>
> **whatever did you do that for?** (annoyance)

Which as an interrogative is not normally combined with **-ever**.

6 RELATIVE PRONOUNS

a) Relative pronouns (except **what**) normally refer to an antecedent. In:

> **she spoke to the man who/that sat beside her**

who/that is the relative pronoun and **the man** the antecedent.

b) *Defining and non-defining*

A relative clause can be either defining or non-defining. If it is defining, it is so closely linked to the antecedent as to be **essential** to the meaning of the complete sentence. If it is non-defining, its link with the antecedent is looser. A non-defining relative clause is rather similar to a parenthesis. Take the following example:

> **he helped the woman who had called out**

This can mean two things: (1) 'he helped the woman who had called out as opposed to those who had not', or (2) 'he helped the woman (and she had called out)'.

In meaning (1) we are dealing with a defining relative clause: the woman has been defined as the one who called out.

In (2) the woman has already been defined (earlier in the conversation), and the relative clause is added as extra, but not essential, information.

It is, however, perhaps not strictly true to say that the sentence as given above could mean two things: non-defining relative clauses are (should be) preceded by a comma, defining ones are not, so, as it stands, the sentence contains a defining relative clause. The corresponding non-defining one would be:

he ran up to the woman, who had called out

It goes without saying that a definition only makes sense if there are two or more possibilities. This means that a relative clause with a one-possibility-only antecedent, such as **my parents** (I can have only one set of parents), is always non-defining:

my parents, who returned last night, are very upset

he went to Godalming, which is a place I don't much care for

The relative pronoun **that** is confined to defining relative clauses. **Who** and **which** can appear in both types.

c) *who/whom/that*

In subject position **who** or **that** are used:

the girl who/that rescued him got a medal

In object position **who(m)** or **that** are used:

the man who(m)/that she rescued was a tourist

Whom is used in more formal language. For more on this see **Interrogative Pronouns**, p 113.

d) *who/which/that*

  i) who/that:

These forms are used for persons and such instances of animals as discussed under **Personal Pronouns** c) above, p 103:

we ignored the people who/that were late

the mouse did not get past Fluffy, who had it in her jaws in no time

Note that only **who** and not **that** can be used in the second example, which is non-defining use, see b) above.

As regards collective nouns, if personal individuality is emphasized, **who** or **that** are preferred. If we are thinking of the unit in a less personal sense, **which** (or **that**) are normal:

the crowd who/that had gathered were in great spirits

the crowd which/that had gathered was enormous

Similarly with names of firms:

you'll find it in Harrods, which is a gigantic store

try Harrods who, I'm sure, will order it for you

  ii) which/that:

Which or **that** are used for non-persons:

the car which/that drove into the back of me

those disks of mine which/that I sent you

Note that, although personal pronouns can be used with means of transport, as discussed in 1c), this usage does not extend to relative pronouns.

e) *whose*

The genitive **whose** is regularly both personal and non-personal and is now more frequent in its non-personal use than **of which**, which is very formal and often considered clumsy:

> **this is the girl whose mother has just died**
>
> **oh, that's that new machine whose cover is damaged**
>
> **the department, whose staff are all over 50, is likely to be closed down**
>
> **these are antiques whose pedigree is immaculate**
>
> **the vehicles, the state of which left a good deal to be desired, had been in use throughout the year**

f) *which*

   i) **Which** is non-personal only:

   > **I received quite a few books for Christmas, which I still haven't read**

   although it can refer to personal characteristics:

   > **she accused him of being an alcoholic, which in fact he is**

   ii) When **which** is bound, it is common only after a preposition and with non-personal reference. Bound **which** is a little formal even after a preposition:

   > **they stayed together for a year, during which time they managed to buy a house and start a family**
   >
   > **he returned to Nottingham, in which city he had been born and bred**

   and very formal if there is no preposition:

   > **he rarely spoke in public, which fact only added to his obscurity**

   and archaic or legal jargon if the antecedent is personal:

   > **Messrs McKenzie and Pirie, which gentlemen have been referred to above ...**

g) *what*

   i) **What** is the only relative without an antecedent. It can be free or bound. When free it is normally non-personal and often has the meaning **that which** or (in the plural) **the things which**:

      show me what did the damage

     When bound it can be both personal and non-personal, corresponding to **the** (+ noun) **who/which**:

      show me what damage was done

      with what volunteers they could find they set off for the summit

      what money they had left, they spent on drink

   ii) **what** or **which**?

     Only **which** can point back to a whole clause since **what** has no antecedent. But **what** can point forward to a clause. Compare:

      she left the baby unattended, which was a silly thing to do

     but:

      she left the baby unattended and what's more, she smacked it when it cried

h) *With -ever*

   Unlike interrogative pronouns, (see above, p 113) **-ever** does not express surprise, confusion or annoyance with relatives; it only adds emphasis in the sense of 'no matter (who, which, what)':

      tell it to whoever you want to

      take whichever (tool) is best

      do whatever you like

      I'll do it whatever happens

      whatever problems we may have to face, we'll solve them

i) *Omission of the relative*

The relative pronoun can be omitted (and very frequently is in spoken English) in defining relative clauses unless it is the subject or is preceded by a preposition:

these are the things we have to do

I saw the boy you met last night

is this the assistant you spoke to?

who's the girl you came to the party with?

she's not the woman she was

Note that only **that** would be inserted in this last example.

Note too that the rather formal construction:

who are the people with whom you are doing business?

can be avoided by a repositioning of the preposition ('with'):

who are the people you are doing business with?

In colloquial spoken English a relative functioning as subject is not infrequently omitted after **there is**, **here is**, **it is**, **that is**:

there's a man wants to speak to you

here's a car will make your eyes pop out

it isn't everybody gets a chance like that

that was her husband just walked by

7 INDEFINITE PRONOUNS

a) *some and any*

i) The combinations with **-body**, **-one**, **-thing** are free (= cannot be followed by a noun) whereas **some** and **any** on their own may be free or bound, singular or plural:

did you speak to anybody?

tell me something

I have some (sugar)

do you have any (friends)?

ii) When a speaker uses **some**, he thinks 'positively' in the sense that he implies or expects the existence of at least a little amount, at least a few objects, animals or persons. When he uses **any**, his thoughts are not conditioned by this positive element. This is why **any** is used in negative clauses and with words implying some form of negation, such as **hardly**:

I haven't got any money, but you have some

I have got hardly any money

Similarly, **any** is frequent in questions and conditions because such clauses are by definition not affirmative:

have you got any money?

if you have any money, give it to me

However, it is misleading to state or imply (as some grammars do) that **some** is infrequent in questions and conditional clauses. It all boils down to the speaker's expectations. Compare:

(a) **have you got some brandy for the pudding?**

(b) **did you bring some sweets for the kids?**

(c) **if you had some milk, you'd feel better**

(d) **if they leave some ice-cream behind, can I have it?**

(e) **have we got any brandy in the house?**

(f) **did you give any sweets to that donkey?**

(g) **if you have had any milk, please tell me**

(h) **if they left any ice-cream behind, I didn't see it**

In (a)-(d) **some** means roughly 'a little' or 'a few', whereas in (e)-(h) **any** implies 'at all' or 'whatever'. For instance, the speaker of (e) wants to know whether there is brandy in the house or not. His mind is not focussing on a certain amount, just enough for a Christmas pudding, as is the case with the person who says (a).

Similarly, **some milk** in (c) means 'a glass of milk' or some such amount, whereas the doctor who uttered (g) was interested in whether his patient had had any milk **at all** (because it might have caused certain symptoms).

iii) **Some/any** versus their combinations:

Compare:

(a) **have they produced any?**

(b) **have they produced anything?**

In (a) the noun that **any** refers to is understood and was mentioned a little earlier; but in (b) there is no such direct reference. A typical context for (a) would be:

they're always going on about how much they like children — have they produced any yet?

whereas for (b) it might be:

the think-tank have been locked away for a week — have they produced anything yet?

Context-bound use of **some** and **any** can also refer to uncountable nouns (in the context example above **any** refers to a countable noun (**children**), which must be plural):

I've run out of coffee, have you got any?

But note context-free **some** in the sense of 'people' or 'those':

there are some who will never learn

iv) **some(thing)/any(thing) + of + noun:**

Some/any before an of-phrase is **quantitative** in meaning whereas **something/anything** + of-phrase is **qualitative**. Compare:

(a) **give me some of that cheese**

(b) **he hadn't lost any of his old style**

(c) **he hadn't lost anything of his old style**

(d) **there is something of the artist in her**

In (a) and (b) **some** and **any** refer to 'a portion, part' whereas in (c) and (d) they correspond to 'anything/something in the way of' or 'anything/something in the nature of'.

v) **some** = an unknown:

We have seen (in ii above) how 'positive' **some** is used with plural nouns (**would you like some biscuits?**) or uncountable nouns (**he stayed here for some time**). With **singular** countable nouns it often means 'an unknown':

some person (or other) must have taken it

he's got some fancy woman in London, it seems

come and see me some time (a different sense of 'time' from the example above)

vi) **some** = 'a poor, bad' or 'a fine, excellent':

In colloquial English **some** is often used in these two senses:

some husband you are! always in the pub with your mates! (= a bad)

this really is some party! (= a great)

vii) Adverbial **some/any**, **something**, **anything**:

Some: before numerals = **about**:

some fifty or sixty people were present

with **more**:

talk to me some more (= a bit more)

in American English:

we talked some (= a bit)

Any is used adverbially before comparatives:

he isn't any less of a friend in spite of this

I refuse to discuss this any further

Before **like**, **something** or **anything** are used adverbially in the sense of 'rather' or 'about' (**something**) and 'at all' (**anything**):

it tasted something like strawberries

something like fifty or sixty people were present (see vii above)

it wasn't anything like I had imagined

Otherwise **something** used as an adverb of degree is colloquial or dialect:

ooh, that baby howls something terrible!

he fancies her something rotten (= very much)

b) *no and none*

i) **No** is bound to a noun:

he has no house, no money, no friends

unless it is used adverbially, in the sense of 'not' before comparatives:

we paid no more than £2 for it

I want £2 for it, no more, no less

The difference between **not** and **no** in such positions is that **not** is more precise, **no** more emotional. **No more than** can be replaced by 'only'. But if a speaker says:

I wish to pay not more than £2

he is pointing out that the price is not to exceed £2.

ii) **None** is free:

do you have any cigarettes? – no, I've none left

I tried a lot but none (of them) fitted

Note that in ordinary spoken English a sentence like:

I have none

often sounds rather formal or dramatic or would be

used for special emphasis. The normal construction would be:

I don't have any

When referring to people **none of them/us/you** is commoner than **none** in spoken English:

none of us knew where he had filed it

I waited for them for hours, but none of them came

many have set out to climb this mountain but none have ever returned

For emphatic usage there is the construction **not one**:

not one (of them) was able to tell me the answer!

iii) **none**: singular or plural:

Since **none** literally means 'no one' some people feel that a singular verb ought to go with it, as in:

none of them has been here before

All the same a plural verb is perfectly normal in everyday spoken (and written) English:

none of them have been here before

iv) Adverbial **none**:

This is used before **the** + a comparative (compare **any** in a) vii above):

none the less (= nevertheless)

you can scratch a CD and they are none the worse for it

he took the medicine but is feeling none the better

after his explanation we were all none the wiser

c) *every and each*

i) **Each** can be both free and bound; **every** bound only. Both refer to countable nouns only:

each (of them) was given a candle

each (child) was given a candle

every child needs a good education

The difference between **every** and **each** is that **every** implies comprehensiveness (there is no exception) whereas **each** individualizes. In the first two examples above **each** implies almost 'one by one'. This is also why **each** often refers to a smaller number than **every**, which generalizes more, as in the third example.

Note that **every** can be preceded by a genitive (noun or pronoun):

Wendy's every move was commented on

her every move was commented on

and note its use with numerals:

they come to stay every three months

every other day there's something wrong

the clock seems to stop every two days

The difference between **every other** and **every two** is that **every other** tends to imply irritation whereas **every two** is more objective and precise.

Note also the adverbial use in:

every now and then

every now and again

every so often

all meaning 'from time to time'.

Everybody/everyone and **everything** are free and all take a singular verb but, like other indefinite pronouns, **everybody** may be followed by **they**, **them(selves)** or **their** (see **Personal Pronouns**, p 106).

d) *All*

i) **All** can be bound or free and refer to both countable and uncountable nouns. When the definite article or a pronoun is used, it comes between **all** and the noun:

all coins are valuable to me

I want all the/those/their coins

all his energy was spent

I want them all/all of them

I want it all/all of it

ii) **all** and **everything**:

The difference between them is often slight. **All** is more likely to be used when the speaker is referring to something specific (compare the difference between **some** and **any** on p 120). Only **all** can refer to uncountable nouns.

we ate everything that was on the table

all that was on the table was a single vase

did you eat the ice-cream? – not all (of it)

they believed everything/all he said

did he say anything? – all that he said was 'do nothing'

iii) **all** and **whole**:

The main difference between **all** and the adjective **whole** is that **whole** is sometimes more emphatically precise:

don't interrupt me all the time

he sat there the whole time without moving

all the assembly gave him a hearty welcome

will this hall hold the whole assembly?

he ate all of the pie

he ate the whole pie

And **whole** is confined to countable nouns:

the whole town (or all the town)

but only:

all the butter (uncountable)

iv) Adverbial **all**:

Adverbial usage is clear in examples like the following, where **all** is equivalent to 'completely':

he was all covered in mud

should we teach her a lesson? — I'm all in favour (of that)

it's all over, honey

Other examples of adverbial **all**:

I've told you all along not to eat the cat's food

he was covered in mud all over

Before comparatives:

I've stopped smoking and feel all the better for it

your remark is all the more regrettable since the Principal was present

e) *other(s) and another*

i) **Another** goes with, or replaces, a singular countable noun. A plural noun can be preceded by **other** only, whereas **others** is always free:

I want another (hamburger)

other children get more money

I like these colours — don't you like the others?

ii) If **than** follows the noun, **other** may follow rather than precede that noun:

there are difficulties other than those noticed by the government

In this sentence **other** could also precede **difficulties** but it is immovable after **none**:

who should arrive? none other than Jimbo himself

iii) Sometimes **no other** is used instead of **not another**:

he always wears that coat; he has no other (coat)

iv) Note constructions with **some** and its combinations,
where **some** means 'an unknown' (compare a) v
above). The addition of **or other** emphasizes 'the
unknown':

somebody or other must have betrayed her

we'll get there somehow or other (adverbial usage)

v) With **one**:

One ... another and **one ... the other** normally mean
the same thing:

one week after another went by

one week after the other went by

But if the speaker refers to two only, then **one ... the
other** is preferred:

**the two brothers worked well together: one would
sweep the yard while the other chopped the wood**

although if the second element is after a preposition,
one ... another is also found even with reference to
only two:

**they would sit there and repeat, one after another,
every single word of the lesson**

Sometimes we find the combination **the one ... the
other**, which could have been used in, for instance, the
example with the two brothers above. In the idiomatic
phrase with **hand**, **the one** is obligatory:

**on the one hand, you'd earn less, on the other your
job satisfaction would be greater**

f) *either and neither*

i) **Either** frequently means 'one or the other' out of two
(we use **any** if there are more than two). It can be
bound as well as free:

'bike' or 'bicycle': either (word) will do

either parent can look after the children

Either may also mean 'each' or 'both', in which case it is bound only:

he was sitting in a taxi with a girl on either side

ii) **Neither** is the negative of **either**:

he's in love with both Tracy and Cheryl, but neither of them fancies him

neither kidney is functioning properly

iii) **Either** and **neither** often take a plural verb if followed by **of** with a plural noun:

(n)either of the boys are likely to have done it

although a singular verb occurs in formal language:

(n)either of the boys is likely to have done it

iv) Adverbial **(n)either**:

Adverbial **either** is confined to negative clauses. It corresponds to **too** in affirmative clauses:

I can't do it either (compare 'I can do it too')

Adverbial **neither** (= nor) is used in a clause **following** a negative clause:

I can't swim and neither can she

I can't swim — neither can I

or colloquially:

I can't swim — me neither

See also **Conjunctions**, p 228.

g) *both*

Both refers to two, but in the sense 'one as well as the other'. As in the case of **all**, the definite article or a pronoun (when used) follows **both**, which can be bound or free:

I like both (those/of those) jackets

we love both our parents

we love both (of them)/them both

both (the/of the) versions are correct

h) *one*

i) This pronoun is used in the sense of 'a single person or thing' just referred to in the previous sentence or clause:

do you like dogs? I bet you haven't ever owned one

we've a lot of records of Elvis — we have only one

his case is a sad one

this solution is one of considerable ingenuity

It can also be used in the plural (**ones**):

I like silk blouses, especially black ones

ii) The definite use can be seen in examples like:

which girl do you prefer? — the tall one

I prefer the pen you gave me to the one my aunt gave me

these are the ones I meant

these burgers are better than the ones you make

iii) **One(s)** is normally used after adjectives referring to countable nouns:

I asked for a large whisky and he gave me a small one

which shoes do you want? — the grey ones?

However, if two contrasting adjectives are close to each other, we sometimes dispense with **one(s)**:

I like all women, both (the) tall and (the) short

she stood by him in good times and bad

today I wish to talk about two kinds of climate, the temperate and the tropical

If no noun has been mentioned, the adjective functions as a noun, in which case **one(s)** is not used:

the survival of the fittest

fortune favours the brave

And it goes without saying that **one** cannot refer to uncountable nouns:

do you want white sugar or brown?

iv) **One** is sometimes used in a sense that gets close to 'somebody' or 'a person', as in:

she screamed her head off like one possessed

I'm not one for big parties

I'm not one to complain

v) Generic **one**, see p 107.

7. VERBS

A. TYPES

We can distinguish three types of verb: regular, irregular and auxiliary.

1 REGULAR VERBS

These form their past tense and past participle by adding **-ed** to the base:

	past tense	*past participle*
seem	**seemed**	**seemed** /d/
kiss	**kissed**	**kissed** /t/
plant	**planted**	**planted** /ɪd/

See p 247 for spelling changes.

2 IRREGULAR VERBS

There are two basic kinds: those that change their vowel, and those that don't.

a) *With vowel changes*

   i) adding **-d** or **-t**:

   hear, heard, heard /ɪə/ /ɜ:/
   keep, kept, kept

   with consonant replacement:

   leave, left, left
   catch, caught, caught

   ii) adding **-(e)n** in the past participle:

   same vowel in past tense and past participle:

   speak, spoke, spoken

same vowel in base and past participle:

see, saw, seen

different vowel sounds in all three forms:

drive, drove, driven

with different base in past tense:

go, went, gone

iii) without any ending:

same vowel in past tense and past participle:

sit, sat, sat
stand, stood, stood (note loss of **-n**)

same vowel in base and past participle:

run, ran, run

different vowel in all three forms:

sing, sang, sung

b) *Without vowel changes*

i) adding **-d** or **-t**:

spoil, spoilt, spoilt

with spelling change:

pay, paid, paid
spill, spilt, spilt

ii) replacing **-d** by **-t**:

send, sent, sent

iii) no change:

cut, cut, cut

iv) the verb 'make':

make, made, made

A list of irregular verbs can be found on p 205.

3 AUXILIARY VERBS

In the same way as an adjective can modify a noun (**the green hat**) so an auxiliary modifies the main verb in the verb phrase. In **he can sing** the auxiliary is **can** and the main verb is **sing**.

We distinguish between 'primary' auxiliaries and 'modal' auxiliaries.

a) *Primary auxiliaries*

These are:

be, **have** and **do**. See also section 23.

We call them 'primary' because they can sometimes function as main verbs as well:

he is singing (**is** = auxiliary, **singing** = main verb)

he is a child (**is** = main verb)

he has sung (**has** = auxiliary, **sung** = main verb)

he has a child (**has** = main verb)

he does not sing (**does** = auxiliary, **sing** = main verb)

he does the washing up (**does** = main verb)

b) Modal auxiliaries are so called because they have in many cases come to replace the subjunctive mood (see p 173). They are:

can – could
may – might
shall – should
will – would
must
ought to

When they are used without a main verb, the main verb is understood:

can you sing? – yes, I can

B. FORMS

1 THE INFINITIVE

For this the base of the verb is used, with or without the word **to** in front of it:

> **he can sing**
>
> **he is trying to sing**

In both these sentences the word **sing** is in the infinitive.

For the infinitive in the perfective aspect and the passive mood, see p 138 and p 139.

2 THE PRESENT PARTICIPLE

This consists of the base + **-ing**:

> **they were whispering**

See **Notes on Spelling** on p 247.

3 THE PAST PARTICIPLE

For regular verbs the form is identical with that of the past tense, ie base + **-ed**:

> **they were kicked**

The irregular verbs have many different forms for the past participle; see A2a) above and the list of irregular verbs on p 205.

4 THE GERUND

This has the same form as the present participle:

> **I don't like picking strawberries**
>
> **sailing is a very popular sport in Greece**

5 THE PRESENT TENSE

This is the base with an added **-(e)s** in the 3rd person singular indicative (for spelling changes see p 247):

	singular		*plural*	
1st	I	**sing**	we	**sing**
2nd	you	**sing**	you	**sing**
3rd	he/she/it	**sings**	they	**sing**

Modal auxiliaries do not change their form in the 3rd person singular, nor do the verbs **dare** and **need** when used as auxiliaries:

he may come

how dare he come here!

he need not sing so loudly

The primary auxiliaries have irregular forms; see the list on p 212.

6 THE PAST TENSE

For regular verbs the form is identical with that of the past participle, ie base + **-ed**:

they kicked the ball

For irregular verbs and auxiliaries, see A2a) and 3 above and the lists of irregular and auxiliary verbs on p 205 – 213. The form of the verb is the same in all persons:

	regular	*irregular*	*auxiliary*
	singular		
1st I	**kissed**	**sang**	**could**
2nd you	**kissed**	**sang**	**could**
3rd he/she/it	**kissed**	**sang**	**could**
	plural		
1st we	**kissed**	**sang**	**could**
2nd you	**kissed**	**sang**	**could**
3rd they	**kissed**	**sang**	**could**

7 TENSE AND ASPECT

The infinitive and the present and past tenses can be combined with 'aspects', which view an event in time. There are three aspects:

simple, continuous and perfect(ive):

infinitive simple	**(to) smoke**
infinitive continuous	**(to) be smoking** (**be** + present participle)
infinitive perfect(ive)	**(to) have smoked** (**have** + past participle)
infinitive perfect(ive) *continuous*	**(to) have been smoking**
present simple	**(I/you/he** etc) **smoke(s)**
past simple	**smoked**
present continuous	**am/are/is smoking**
past continuous	**was/were smoking**
present perfect(ive)	**have/has smoked**
past perfect(ive)	**had smoked**
present perfect(ive) continuous	**have/has been smoking**
past perfect(ive) continuous	**had been smoking**

The 'continuous' is sometimes called the 'progressive'; and some (older) grammars refer to the 'present perfect' as the 'perfect', and the 'past perfect' as the 'pluperfect'.

For forms used for the future see p 165.

8 MOOD

Mood refers to the speaker's (or writer's) attitude to the factual content of his utterance. There are three moods:

the 'indicative' for reality and fact

the 'subjunctive' for wish, uncertainty, possibility and the like the 'imperative' for commands and suggestions.

The only difference in form between the indicative and the subjunctive is the **-(e)s** in the 3rd singular person indicative — this is not added in the subjunctive:

> **God save the Queen!**

The subjunctive of **be** is **be** in all persons of the present and **were** in all persons of the past:

> **home is home, be it ever so humble**
>
> **if I were you, I'd leave him**

For the imperative mood the base form is used:

> **ring the bell!**
>
> **somebody go and get it!**

9 VOICE

The two 'voices' are the 'active' and the 'passive'. They indicate whether the subject of a verb performs the action of that verb, as in:

> **he drives** (active)

or whether the subject is the 'victim' of the action or has the action done **to** him/her, as in:

> **he was driven (by his wife)** (passive)

The passive is formed with the verb **be** + the past participle:

infinitive simple	**(to) be smoked**
infinitive perfect(ive)	**(to) have been smoked**
present simple	**are/is smoked**
past simple	**was/were smoked**
present continuous	**are/is being smoked**
past continuous	**was/were being smoked**
present perfect(ive)	**have/has been smoked**
past perfect(ive)	**had been smoked**

present perfect(ive)	**have/has been being**
continuous	**smoked**
past perfect(ive) continuous	**had been being smoked**

The passive of the infinitive continuous (eg **to be being driven**) is fairly unusual in English (though perfectly possible):

I wouldn't like to be being filmed looking like this

Similarly with the passive perfect continuous:

he may have been being operated on by then

C. USE

1 THE INFINITIVE

a) *Without to*

   i) after modal auxiliaries and **do**:

   I must go
   I don't know

   ii) after **dare** and **need** when used as auxiliaries:

   how dare you talk to me like that!
   you needn't talk to me like that

   iii) after **had better** and **had best** (also **would best** in American English):

   you had better apologize
   you had (you'd) best ask the porter

   iv) in the so-called 'accusative with infinitive' construction (= noun/pronoun + infinitive functioning together as object); compare b) ii below:

   * after **let**, **make** and **have** (see also p 184):

   we let him smoke
   I made him turn round
   we had him say a few words

* after the following verbs of sense perception:

feel, **hear**, **see**, **watch**:

I felt the woman touch my back

we heard her tell the porter

they saw him die

we watched the train approach the platform

For **feel** as a 'point of view' verb, see b) ii below.

These verbs can also be followed by the present participle. The difference between them corresponds to the difference in usage between the simple and the continuous aspects, for which see p 161:

I felt her creeping up behind me

we heard her crying bitterly in the next room

she saw smoke coming from the house

they watched him slowly dying

* two infinitive forms are possible after **help**:

we helped him (to) move house

This is also true without the 'accusative', the **to**-less infinitive being particularly common in advertising language:

our soap helps keep your skin supple and healthy-looking

For the corresponding passive constructions with these verbs, see b) ii below.

v) after **why (not)**:

why stay indoors in this lovely weather?

why not try our cream cakes?

b) *With to*

i) The infinitive with **to** can be used as the subject, complement or object of a sentence. The following example contains all three (in that order):

to die is to cease to exist

ii) In an accusative with infinitive; compare a) iv above.

* After verbs expressing desire or dislike, especially **want**, **wish**, **like**, **prefer**, **hate**:

I want/wish you to remember this

John would like you to leave

we prefer your cousin to stay here

we would hate our cat to suffer

* In fairly formal language after 'point of view' verbs expressing belief, supposition, judgement, assertiveness:

we believe this to be a mistake

we supposed him to be dead

we considered/judged it to be of little use

I felt/knew it to be true

these accusations he maintained to be false

Less formal language would prefer a **that**-clause:

we believe (that) this is a mistake

I know (that) it's true

he maintained that these accusations were false

* In the corresponding passive construction **to** remains:

this was believed to be a mistake

* Note the common **be said to**, for which there is no active equivalent:

it is said to be true

* The **to**-infinitive must also be used in passive constructions with the verbs in a) iv above:

she was made to do it

he was seen to remove both jacket and tie

iii) Used following nouns, pronouns and adjectives:

she has always had a tendency to become hysterical

we shall remember this in days to come

there are things to be done

there is that to take into consideration

glad to meet you!

we were afraid to ask

this game is easy to understand

Such constructions are particularly common after superlatives and **only**:

this is the latest book to appear on the subject

she's the only person to have got near him

iv) Corresponding to a subordinate clause:

* Expressing purpose or result (sometimes with the addition of **in order** or **so as** (purpose) or **only** (result) for emphasis):

he left early (in order/so as) to get a good seat

they arrived (only) to find an empty house

try to be there

Note that in spoken English **to** after 'try' can be replaced by **and**:

try and be there

* With embedded interrogatives:

tell me what to do

I didn't know where to look

we didn't know who to ask

we weren't sure whether to tell him or not

* Expressing time or circumstance:

  I shudder to think of it (= when I think of it)

  to hear him speak, one would think he positively hates women (= when one hears him speak ...)

v) Corresponding to a main clause, in exclamations of surprise:

  to think she married him! (= it's strange to think ...)

vi) In elliptical sentences expressing future arrangements. These are typical of newspaper headlines:

  MAGGIE TO MAKE GREEN SPEECH

  GORBACHEV TO VISIT DISASTER ZONE

vii) The 'split infinitive', so called because an adverb is put between **to** and the base, has become very common in spite of being frowned upon by many:

  nobody will ever be able to fully comprehend his philosophy

  However, it can sometimes be the natural position for an adverb:

  the way out of this is to really try and persuade him

  Here **really** means 'very much' and modifies **try**, whereas in the next sentence **really** could also mean 'actually' and thus modify the whole sentence:

  the way out of this is really to try and persuade him

viii) **To** without the base is often used in repetition rather than the complete infinitive:

  why haven't you tidied your room? I told you to

  I did it because she encouraged me to

ix) **For** + noun/pronoun and **to**- infinitive:

  there has always been a tendency for our language to absorb foreign words

  he waited for her to finish

This idiomatic construction often expresses condition or purpose:

for the university to function properly, more money is needed

or it can express circumstance and even be the subject of the sentence:

for me to say nothing would be admitting defeat

for a man to get custody of his children used to be difficult

2 THE GERUND

The gerund (or verbal noun) has features typical of both nouns and verbs.

a) *Noun-like features*

i) A gerund can be subject, complement or object:

skating is difficult (subject)

that is cheating (complement)

I hate fishing (object)

As we have seen, these are functions that are shared with the infinitive; for differences in usage, see 4 below.

ii) It can follow a preposition:

he's thought of leaving

The infinitive cannot occupy this position.

iii) It can be modified by an article, adjective or a possessive, and be post-modified by a phrase beginning with **of**:

he has always recommended the reading of good literature

he deserves a beating

careless writing leaves a bad impression

the soprano's singing left us unmoved

the timing of his remarks was unfortunate

b) *Verb-like features*

i) A gerund can take an object or a complement:

hitting the dog was unavoidable

becoming an expert took him more than twenty years

ii) It can be modified by an adverbial:

she was afraid of totally disillusioning him

iii) It can have a subject:

the idea of John going to see her is absurd

3   THE POSSESSIVE AND THE GERUND

There is often uncertainty about the presence or absence of a possessive:

do you remember him/his trying to persuade her?

Here both are correct. But this does not mean that there is never any difference in usage between the two. The following instances are worthy of note:

a) *The gerund as subject or complement*

Here the possessive is normal:

your trying to persuade me will get you nowhere

it was John's insisting we went there that saved the situation

b) *The gerund as object or following a preposition*

In such cases both uses are possible:

they spoke at great length about him/his being elected president

you don't mind me/my turning up so late, do you?

they spoke at great length about Richard/Richard's being elected president

But there are cases when the use of the possessive would present something of a style clash in spoken or colloquial contexts:

they laughed their heads off at him falling into the river

The use of the possessive 'his' would be too formal in this example.

In these constructions the gerund must not be confused with the present participle. The sentence:

I hate people trying to get in without paying

is potentially ambiguous. If **trying** is a gerund, the meaning is 'I hate the fact that (some) people try to get in without paying'. If it is a present participle, the meaning is 'I hate people who try to get in without paying'.

But the **-ing** form is, of course, unambiguously a gerund in a sentence such as:

I hate their trying to get in without paying

There is a tendency to make greater use of the possessive before the gerund in American English than in British English.

c) *The stress factor*

If the subject of the gerund is being heavily emphasized the possessive is less likely to be used:

imagine YOU marrying John!

4 THE GERUND AND THE INFINITIVE COMPARED

a) *Little or no difference*

We have seen that the infinitive and the gerund have noun-like features in that both can function as subject, object and complement. Often there is little or no difference between them in meaning:

we can't bear seeing you like this
we can't bear to see you like this

although of course sayings or quotations are 'fixed', as in the next two examples:

> **seeing is believing**
>
> **to err is human, to forgive divine**

b) *Different meanings*

   i) The general versus the specific: the gerund often indicates a general activity, the infinitive a more specific one:

> **I hate refusing offers like that** (general)
>
> **I hate to refuse an offer like that** (specific)

But there are exceptions:

> **I prefer being called by my Christian name**
>
> **I prefer to be called by my Christian name**

Both of these examples could be either used in a general or a specific context, the difference being academic in any case since a preference is a general thing.

In American English the infinitive is often used in cases where British English would use a gerund:

> **I like cooking** (British)
>
> **I like to cook** (American)

Both of these refer to a general liking. For reference to specific occasions both British and American English would say:

> **I'd like to cook something for you**

  ii) If the verb **try** means 'attempt', either the infinitive or the gerund is used:

> **I once tried to make a film, but I couldn't**
>
> **I once tried making a film, but I couldn't**
>
> **try to speak more slowly**
>
> **try speaking more slowly**

But if **try** is used to mean 'experience', then only the gerund is used:

I've never tried eating shark

Compare this with:

I once tried to eat shark, but couldn't

iii) After **forget** and **remember** the infinitive refers to future time, the gerund to past time, in relation to the 'forgetting' and 'remembering':

I won't forget to dance with her (in the future)

I won't forget dancing with her (in the past)

will she remember to meet me? (in the future)

will she remember meeting me? (in the past)

c) *The infinitive only or the gerund only*

i) The infinitive only:

Some verbs can be followed only by the infinitive, eg **want, wish, hope, deserve**:

I want/wish to leave

we hope to be back by five

he deserves to be punished

ii) The gerund only:

Other verbs take the gerund only, eg **avoid, consider, dislike, enjoy, finish, keep, practise, risk**:

he avoided answering my questions

I dislike dressing up for the theatre

we enjoy having friends round to dinner

she finished typing her letter

why do you keep reminding me?

would you mind stepping this way, Sir?

you must practise playing the piano more often

I don't want to risk upsetting Jennifer

iii) In the examples in the two sections above both the infinitive and the gerund are objects of the preceding verb. So is the gerund in:

I stopped looking at her

but not the infinitive in:

I stopped to look at her

Here the infinitive functions as an adverbial of purpose, which explains the considerable difference in meaning between the two sentences. The difference is equally great between:

he was too busy talking to her (ie talking made him busy)

and

he was too busy to talk to her (ie he was busy doing something else)

Here it might be worth noting that the adjectives **worth** and **like** can be followed by the gerund only:

that suggestion is worth considering

that's just like wishing for the moon

iv) It is also important to distinguish between **to** as a marker of the infinitive and as a preposition. The gerund must follow a preposition, as in:

I'm tired of watching television

what do you think about getting a loan?

This, of course, applies to the preposition **to** as well:

they are committed to implementing the plan

we're looking forward to receiving your letter

I object to raising money for that purpose

we're not used to getting up at this hour

Be accustomed to is sometimes found with the infinitive, though:

they've never been accustomed to pay(ing) for anything

5   THE PRESENT PARTICIPLE

A present participle normally functions either as a verb or as an adjective.

a)   *Functioning as a verb*

i)   The present participle is used with **be** to form the continuous (see B7):

he is/was/has been/had been running

ii)   The present participle frequently functions as an elliptical relative clause:

they went up to the people coming from the theatre (= who were coming)

iii)   However, it may have a looser connection with the rest of the sentence, sharing its subject with the verb in the present or past tense. In writing, the looser connection is often indicated by a comma, in speech by intonation:

she turned towards the man, looking shy and afraid

Here the subject of **looking** is **she**; but if we leave out the comma, the subject of **looking** is likely to be interpreted as **the man**, and the sentence would then belong to the type in ii above.

This relatively loose present participle may precede its subject:

looking shy and afraid, she turned towards the man

It often expresses cause, condition or time, being equivalent to a subordinate clause:

living alone, she often feels uneasy at night (= because/since/as she lives alone . . .)

you'd get more out of life, living alone (= . . . if you lived alone)

driving along, I suddenly passed a field of tulips (= as/while I was driving along . . .)

But sometimes it is equivalent to a main clause:

she went up to him, asking for his advice (= . . .and (she) asked for his advice)

living in the Scottish Highlands, he is a sensitive musician who helped organize the Bath Orchestra (= he lives in the Highlands and (he) is . . .)

iv) The 'dangling' participle:

A present participle is considered to be 'dangling' if its subject is other than that of the verb in the present or past tense:

coming down the staircase carrying an umbrella, one of the mice tripped him up

It is unlikely that the subject of **coming** is **one of the mice**! 'Dangling' participles are normally to be avoided as they often cause unintentional amusement. However, if an indefinite subject is understood, like an indefinite **we** or French **on** or German **man**, then a 'dangling' participle is acceptable:

generally speaking, British cooking leaves a good deal to be desired

judging by the way she dresses, she must have a lot of confidence

the work will have to be postponed, seeing that only two of us have tools

v) In other circumstances, to avoid a 'dangling' participle, the subject of the participle (different from that of the other verb) can precede it in the so-called 'absolute construction':

the lift being out of order, we had to use the stairs

she being the hostess, any kind of criticism was out of the question

we'll do it on Sunday, weather permitting

God willing, we can do it

b)   *Functioning as an adjective*:

>   **she has always been a loving child**
>   **her appearance is striking**
>   **she finds Henry very charming**

From this function comes the adverbial one:

>   **he is strikingly handsome**

6   THE PRESENT PARTICIPLE AND THE GERUND COMPARED

a)   Take the following sentence:

>   **I can't get used to that man avoiding my eyes all the time**

This is ambiguous because **avoiding** can be interpreted as either a gerund or a present participle.

If it is a gerund, the sentence is equivalent to 'I can't get used to the fact that that man is avoiding my eyes'.

But if it is a present participle, the meaning is 'I can't get used to that man who is avoiding my eyes'.

In the following sentence there is no doubt that the **-ing** form is a gerund:

>   **children suffering like that is on our conscience** (= the suffering of children)

nor is there any doubt that it is a present participle in:

>   **children suffering like that are on our conscience** (= children who suffer)

b)   When a gerund modifies a noun, only the gerund is stressed in speech; the noun is not:

>   **a living room** (= room for living)

but when the modifier is a present participle, it and the noun receive equal stress:

>   **a living animal** (= an animal that lives/is alive)

7 THE PAST PARTICIPLE

Many of the following functions should be compared with those of the present participle; see 5 above.

a) *Functioning as a verb*

i) The past participle is used with **have** to form the perfective aspect:

he has/had arrived

and with **be** to form the passive voice:

she is/was admired

and with both to form the perfective passive:

she has/had been admired

ii) The past participle frequently functions as an elliptical relative clause:

they ignore the concerts given by the local orchestra
(= which are given)

they ignored the concerts given by the local orchestra
(= which were/had been given)

Or it can function as a subordinate clause of cause, condition or time. A conjunction (especially **if** and **when**) sometimes makes the meaning explicit:

watched over by her family, Monica felt safe but unhappy

(if) treated with care, records should last for years and years

records should last for years and years if treated with care

(when) asked why this was so, he refused to answer

he refused to answer when asked why this was so

Or it can function as a main clause:

born in Aberdeen, he now lives in Perth with his wife and children

iii) The past participle sometimes 'dangles' unacceptably by becoming detached from the subject of the sentence:

told to cancel the meeting, his project was never discussed

This could be better expressed as:

his project was never discussed as he was told to cancel the meeting

iv) The 'absolute construction' (see 5a) v above):

the problems solved, they went their separate ways

that done, he left

b) *Functioning as an adjective*

I am very tired

the defeated army retreated

Note that in the first example the modifier is **very**, as indeed it must be before an adjective. If the modifier is **much**, the verb-like character of the past participle is emphasized:

I am much obliged

he's been much troubled by the news

When **aged, beloved, blessed, cursed** and **learned** are adjectives, -**ed** is normally pronounced /ɪd/; but when they are verbs, the pronunciation is the regular /d/ and/t/:

he has aged

an aged man /ɪd/

he comes here every blessed night! /ɪd/

this cursed family of his will stop at nothing /ɪd/

8 QUESTIONS

a) *Complete sentences*

i) **Do** is used for questions unless (a) the clause contains another auxiliary (**have**, **will** etc), in which case the auxiliary precedes the subject, or (b) the subject is an interrogative pronoun. **Do** is in the present or past tense, the main verb in the infinitive:

do you come here often?

how do we get to Oxford Street from here?

did you see that girl?

what did you say?

but (other auxiliary being used):

are they trying to speak to us?

where are you taking me?

have they seen us?

can you come at eight?

will you help?

what have they said to you?

what shall we write about?

and (interrogative pronoun as subject):

who said that?

what happened?

For **dare** and **need**, see p 196. For **have**, see p 181.

ii) In spoken English, where intonation distinguishes interrogative clauses from affirmative ones, questions can be asked using the word order of affirmative clauses:

you just left him standing there?

you're coming tonight?

In indirect questions affirmative word order is normally used. Compare:

when are you leaving? (direct question)

and

he asked her when she was leaving (indirect question)

b) *Question-tags*

These are short questions following an affirmative or negative clause, and normally asking for confirmation.

i) An affirmative clause is followed by a negative tag and vice versa:

you can see it, can't you?

you can't see it, can you?

unless the tag expresses an emphatic attitude (possessive or negative, as the case may be) rather than a question. In such cases, an affirmative tag follows an affirmative clause:

so you've seen a ghost, have you? (disbelief or sarcasm)

you think that's fair, do you? (resentment)

you've bought a new car, have you? (surprise or interest)

Note that the question tag copies the tense of the main clause:

you want to meet him, don't you?

you wanted to meet him, didn't you?

you'll want to meet him, won't you?

ii) If the preceding clause has an auxiliary, that auxiliary is repeated in the tag:

you have seen it before, haven't you?

they aren't running away, are they?

you will help me, won't you?

you oughtn't to say that, ought you?

In the last case, however, the tag could also take the auxiliary **did**:

he oughtn't to have said that, did he?

as use of **ought he** could sound rather formal.

If there is no auxiliary in the preceding clause, the tag normally has **do**:

he sleeps in there, doesn't he?

your cousin arrived last night, didn't she?

unless the tag follows an imperative, in which case an affirmative auxiliary is used (especially **will/would**). Such tags often prevent abruptness:

leave the cat alone, will you?

take this to Mrs Brown, would you?

In such cases the negative **won't** indicates an invitation:

help yourselves to drinks, won't you?

9 NEGATIONS

a) *Negation of tense forms*

i) **Do** with **not** is used unless the clause contains another auxiliary. In spoken English and informal written English, contraction with auxiliaries is normal (**won't, can't, don't** etc):

we do not/don't accept traveller's cheques

but (another auxiliary in use):

the matter should not/shouldn't be delayed

ii) In negative questions **not** follows the subject unless it has been contracted:

do they not accept traveller's cheques? (but: **don't they accept ...?**)

should you not try this office number? (but: **shouldn't you try ...?**)

iii) The 'point-of-view' verbs **believe, suppose, think** etc are normally negated even if the negation logically belongs with the verb in the object clause:

I don't believe we have met

I don't suppose you could lend me a fiver?

I didn't think these papers were yours

but **hope** follows logic:

I hope it won't give me a headache

and does not even take **do** when it is on its own:

is she ill? — I hope not

A mixture of forms is possible in short answers with **believe, suppose** and **think**:

will she marry him? — I don't believe/think so (common)

I believe/think not (less common, more formal)

I don't suppose so (common)

I suppose not (common)

b) *Negation of infinitives and gerunds*

This is done by putting **not** in front of the infinitive or the gerund:

we tried not to upset her

I want you to think seriously about not going

not eating enough vegetables is a common cause of . . .

The infinitive example above is, of course, quite different in meaning from:

we didn't try to upset her

where a tense-form is being negated.

Note the idiomatic phrase **not to worry = don't worry**:

I won't manage to finish it by tomorrow — not to worry

The infinitive can be split by **not** in colloquial language (**we tried to not upset her**), though this is frowned upon by many, see p 144.

c) *Negation of imperatives*

  i) With **do**. **Do not** is contracted to **don't**:

  don't worry

  don't be silly

  Use of the full form **do not** is common in official statements, instructions, public notices etc:

  do not fill in this part of the form

  do not feed the animals

  do not exceed the stated dose

  The full form can also be used to issue a more emphatic imperative in spoken English:

  I'll say it again — do not touch!

  In the **let's** form of the imperative, used for making suggestions, the word order is:

  don't let's wait any longer

  ii) There is another way of negating the imperative using only the word **not** placed after the verb. This is either biblical or Shakespearean English or can be used for comic effect or sarcasm:

  worry not, I'll be back soon

  fear not, the situation is under control

  But it is normal with **let's**:

  let's not wait any longer

d) **Never** does not normally take **do** with lets:

  we never accept traveller's cheques

  I never said a word

But if a sentence is being said with emphasis then **do** can be used:

> **you never did like my cooking, did you?**

If there is an inversion of auxiliary and subject **do** is used:

> **never did it taste so good!**

> **never did their courage waver**

In the first of these two examples the sentence is more an exclamation than a negation, and in the second the style is poetic or rhetorical.

10 EXPRESSING PRESENT TIME

Present time can be expressed in various ways according to whether we wish to refer to habitual or general events, or to specific events, and whether the latter are seen as ongoing processes or more immediate happenings. This section describes the uses of the relevant verb forms.

a) *The present simple*

i) For habitual or general events and 'eternal truths':

> **I get up at seven o'clock every morning**

> **Mrs Parfitt teaches French at the local school**

> **the earth revolves round the sun**

ii) With verbs that cannot be thought of as referring to a certain time-span or being 'process'-like. Such verbs are sometimes called 'stative' and often express desire/dislike, point of view, or refer to the senses:

> **I (dis)like/love/hate/want that girl**

> **I believe/suppose/think you're right**

> **we hear/see/feel the world around us**

> **it tastes/smells good**

Note that some of these verbs can turn from 'stative' to 'dynamic', implying 'process' or continuity of action. In such cases the present continuous is used:

> **what are you thinking about?**

we're not seeing a lot of him these days

are you not feeling well today?

we're tasting the wine to see if it's all right

b) *The present continuous*

i) The present continuous is used with 'dynamic' verbs, ie verbs that refer to an ongoing, normally temporary, event:

don't interrupt while I'm talking to somebody else

please be quiet; I'm watching a good programme

he's trying to get the car to start

not now, I'm thinking

Compare:

I live in London (present simple)

I'm living in London (present continuous)

The second sentence implies that the speaker is not permanently based in London, that living there is only temporary.

ii) In the light of a) i above, it is obvious that adverbs referring to habitual or general/universal time are frequent with the present simple, as in:

he always goes to bed after midnight

Such use of the present simple stresses the factual content of the utterance. But sometimes the present continuous is used with such adverbs, especially **always** and **forever**, when we wish to express not only the fact itself but also an attitude to it, especially an attitude of irritation, mild amusement or surprise:

you're always saying that! (irritation)

he's always criticizing me (resentment)

John is forever bumping into old ladies (mild amusement)

I'm always finding you here at Betty's (surprise)

11 EXPRESSING PAST TIME

a) *The past simple*

We use this when we want to emphasize the completion of an action or event in the past, often at a specific time indicated by an adverbial:

he caught the train yesterday

he didn't say a word at the meeting

Maria Callas sang at the Lyric Opera only a few times (ie during her lifetime, which is now over)

b) *used to/would*

When we refer to habitual events in the past, we often use **used to** or **would**:

on Sundays we used to go to my grandmother's

on Sundays we would go to my grandmother's

c) *The past continuous*

This stresses the continuity of an action or event:

what were you doing last night around 9 o'clock? — I was repairing the garage door

I was watching my favourite programme when the telephone rang

In the second example **was watching** (past continuous) contrasts with **rang** (past simple). The two verbs contrast in a different way in the next example, in which verb forms have been reversed:

I watched his face while the telephone was ringing

Here the speaker wants to emphasize the 'watching' as a fact that took place at a certain time. He therefore ignores the element of 'process' that the verb might imply, stressing instead the continuity of the 'ringing'. Both examples illustrate the use of the past continuous for events that serve as a background or backdrop to more immediate happenings, for which the simple aspect is preferred.

d) *The present perfect(ive) (continuous)*

We use the present perfect for past actions or events that have some relevance for the present:

she has read an enormous number of books (ie she is very well-read)

Compare the present perfect and the past simple in the following pairs of sentences:

have you heard the news this morning? (it is still morning)

did you hear the news this morning? (said in the afternoon or evening)

he has just arrived (he is here now)

he arrived a moment ago (emphasis on when in the past)

Mrs Smith has died (she is dead)

Mrs Smith died a lonely woman (when she died, she was lonely)

To stress the continuity of an action, the continuous aspect can be used:

I've been living in this city for 10 years

although here the simple form can also be used with the same meaning:

I've lived in this city for 10 years

Note the use of **since** when the reference is to a point in time:

I've been living here since 1971

There are cases, however, when the use of the continuous differs in implication from the use of the simple form. Compare:

I've been waiting for you for three whole hours!

I've waited for you for three whole hours!

The second sentence would not be said directly to the person for whom you had been waiting when this person eventually showed up. But you could say it to that person on the telephone, implying that you are now going to stop waiting.

The first sentence could be said to the person eventually turning up as well as to that person over the telephone.

e) *The past perfect(ive) (continuous)*

This describes actions or events in the past which took place before other happenings in the past. It expresses one past time in relation to another past time:

she had left when I arrived (= by the time I arrived)

she left when I arrived (= as soon as I arrived)

The continuous aspect stresses continuity of action:

she had been trying to get hold of me for hours when I finally turned up

I had been meaning to contact him for ages

For the past perfect in clauses of condition, see p 172.

12 EXPRESSING FUTURE TIME

a) *will and shall*

i) When the speaker is referrring to the future in the 1st person **will** or **shall** can be used. **Will** can be contracted to **'ll. Shall**, however, is mainly British English:

I will/I'll/I shall inform Mr Thompson of her decision

we won't/shan't be long

I will/I'll/I shall be in Rome when you're getting married

ii) In other persons **will** is used:

you will/you'll be surprised when you see him

he will/he'll get angry if you tell him this

iii) If the speaker is expressing an intention in the 2nd or 3rd person (often through promise or threat), **shall** is sometimes found, but is no longer as common as **will**:

you shall get what I promised you

they shall pay for this!

If the intention or willingness is not the speaker's, **will** ('**ll**) is used:

he will/he'll do it, I'm sure

iv) **Shall** is used to make suggestions:

shall we go?   **shall I do it for you?**

In these two examples **will** would not be used.

v) **Will** is used to make requests:

will you step this way, please?

vi) offering, making statements about the immediate future:

In the following examples **will** is used rather than **shall** (although the contracted form is by far the most common occurrence):

leave that, I'll do it

what's it like? — I don't know, I'll try it

try some, you'll like it

there's the phone — ok, I'll answer it

b) *Future simple and future continuous*

i) continuity of action:

If **will** and **shall** are followed by the continuous, it may be because the speaker wishes to stress continuity of action:

I'll be marking essays and you'll be looking after the baby

ii) requests as against questions:

The continuous can also be used to make it clear that the speaker is talking merely in a neutral way about a state of affairs and wants to reduce the volitional force that could be implied by the simple aspect. This is why **will/shall** + infinitive continuous is often found in sentences implying pre-arrangement:

she'll be giving two concerts in London next week (= she is due to give . . .)

will you be bringing that up at the meeting? (is that what's going to happen?)

The question:

will you bring that up at the meeting?

is more likely to be understood as a request to do so rather than as a question as to what you intend to do.

c) *be going to*

i) There is often no difference between **be going to** and **will**:

I wonder if this engine is ever going to start (. . . will ever start)

you're going to just love it (you'll just love it)

what's he going to do about it? (what'll he do about it?)

ii) In statements of intent **be going to** is commoner than **will** or **shall**:

we're going to sell the house after all

he's going to sue

I'm going to go to London tomorrow

But in a longer sentence containing other adverbials and clauses **will** is also possible:

look, what I'll do is this, I'll go to London tomorrow, talk to them about it and . . .

iii) **Be going to** is used in preference to **will** when the reasons for the predictions relate directly to the present:

it's going to rain (look at those clouds)

I know what you're going to say (it's written all over your face)

d) *The present simple*

   i) In main clauses this expresses the future according to a fixed programme. It is particularly common when we make reference to a time-table:

   when does university start? — classes start on October 6th

   the train for London leaves at 11 am

   ii) It is normally used in adverbial clauses of time or condition:

   you'll like him when you see him

   if he turns up, will you speak to him?

   Such **when**- and **if**-clauses must not be confused with interrogative object clauses. In these **when** means 'at what time?' and **if** means 'whether'; and the verb form is that of the corresponding direct question:

   do you know when dad's taking the dog out? (when is dad taking the dog out?)

   I wonder if she'll be there (will she be there?)

e) *The present continuous*

   i) The present continuous is often very similar to **be going to** in expressing intention:

   I'm taking this book with me (I'm going to take this book with me)

   what are you doing over Christmas? (what are you going to do over Christmas?)

ii) But when intention is less prominent, the present
continuous tends to imply pre-arrangement, thus being
similar in use to **will** + infinitive continuous or the
present simple:

> **she's giving two concerts in London next week**

> **the train for London is leaving soon**

f) *be to*

Be to is often used to express specific plans for the future,
especially plans made for us by other people or by fate:

> **the President is to visit the disaster zone** (for headline
> usage see p 144)

> **we are to be there by ten o'clock**

> **are we to meet again, I wonder?**

g) *be about to*

This expresses imminent future:

> **you are about to meet a great artist** (very shortly you
> will meet a great artist)

> **the play is about to start** (any second now)

It can also be used to express intentions about the future
in a usage commoner in American English:

> **I'm not about to let him use my car after what
> happened last time**

British English would be more likely to use **be going to**.

h) *The future perfect(ive) (continuous)*

This is used for an action that will have been completed
(before another action) in the future:

> **by the time we get there he will already have left**

> **by then we'll have been working on this for 5 years**

It is also used for assumptions about the present or past:

> **you'll have been following developments, no doubt**

13 EXPRESSING CONDITION

In conditional sentences the condition is expressed in a subordinate clause placed before or after the main clause and normally starting with **if**:

if the train is late, we'll miss our plane

we'll miss our plane if the train is late

For negative conditions **unless** (= if not) is sometimes used:

unless the train is on time, we'll miss our plane

if the train isn't on time, we'll miss our plane

Since the action of the main clause is dependent on the condition of the subordinate clause, that action must be in the future in relation to the condition (for exceptions see a) i below). The auxiliary that comes nearest to a pure future is **will**, which, together with its past tense **would**, are used in the examples illustrating the uses of conditional sentences.

a) *Reference to present/future time*

i) likely possibility:

The verb of the subordinate clause is in the present tense or in the present perfect. The main clause has **will** + infinitive: (sometimes **shall** + infinitive in the 1st person):

if you see her, you will not recognize her

if you are sitting comfortably, we will begin

if you have completed the forms, I will send them off

if he comes back, I shall ask him to leave

There are three important exceptions:

* When the verb of the main clause is also in the present tense, an automatic or habitual result is normally

implied. In such sentences **if** has almost the meaning of **when(ever)**:

if the sun shines, people look happier

if people eat rat poison, they often die

if you're happy, I'm happy

if you don't increase your offer, you don't get the house

* When **will** is used also in the subordinate clause, the speaker refers to a person's willingness or intention to do something:

if you will be kind enough to stop singing, we will/shall be able to get some sleep

if you will insist on eating all that fatty food you will have to put up with the consequences

When this form is used to make requests the sentence can be made more polite by using **would**:

if you would be kind enough to stop singing, we would/should be able to get some sleep

* When **should** is used in the subordinate clause (in all persons), the condition is implied to be less likely. Such **should**-clauses are often followed by the imperative, as in the first two of the following examples:

if you should see him, ask him to call

if he should turn up, try and avoid him

if they should attack you, you will have to fight them

In a slightly more formal style **if** can be deleted and the sentence started with the subordinate clause with **should**:

should the matter arise again, telephone me at once

ii) unlikely or unreal possibility:

'Unlikely or unreal possibility' means that the condition is expected not to take place or is opposed to known facts. The verb in the subordinate clause is in the past tense; the main clause has **would** (also **should** in the first person) + infinitive:

if you saw her, you would not recognize her

if she had a car, she would visit you more often

if I won that amount, I would/should just spend it all

if the lift was working properly, there would not be so many complaints

This sentence type need not always indicate unlikely or unreal possibility. Often there is little difference between it and the type in a) i above:

if you tried harder, you would pass the exam (if you try harder, you will pass the exam)

The use of the past tense may make the utterance a little friendlier or more polite.

b) *Reference to past time*

i) In such cases there can be no fulfilment of the condition, since what is expressed in the **if**-clause did not take place. The verb of the subordinate clause is in the past perfect; the main clause has **would** (also **should** in the first person) + infinitive perfect:

if you had seen her, you would not have recognized her

if I had been there, I would/should have ignored him

In a slightly more formal style we can delete **if** and start the subordinate clause with **had**:

had I been there, I would/should have ignored him

ii) exceptions:

* If the main clause refers to present unfulfilment of a past condition, **would** + infinitive (simple) can also be used:

if I had studied harder, I would be an engineer today (= if I had studied harder, I would have been an engineer today)

* The past tense is used in both clauses if, as in a) i above, an automatic or habitual result is implied (**if** = **when(ever)**):

if people had influenza in those days, they died

if they tried to undermine the power of the Church, they were burned at the stake

* If the condition is expected to have taken place, the restrictions on verb-form sequences in a) and b) above are lifted. In such cases **if** often means 'as' or 'since'. Note for instance the variety of verb forms in the main clauses following the **if**-clauses (which are all in the past tense):

if he was rude to you, why did you not walk out?

if he was rude to you, why have you still kept in touch?

if he was rude to you, why do you still keep in touch?

if he told you that, he was wrong

if he told you that, he has broken his promise

if he told you that, he is a fool

14 THE SUBJUNCTIVE

As opposed to the indicative, which stresses the factual, the subjunctive implies the non-factual, such as wish, hope, possibility and the like (see under **Mood** p 138).

The present subjunctive is identical in form with the infinitive (without **to**) in all three persons, singular and plural. That is to say, the only way in which the present subjunctive differs in form from the present indicative is in the 3rd person singular, where the **-s** is dropped.

The past subjunctive is marked in form only in the 1st and 3rd persons singular of the verb **to be**, which is **were** although in non-formal language **was** is preferred (see also b) vi below).

a) *The subjunctive in main clauses*

Here the subjunctive is confined to fixed expressions of hoping or wishing, as in:

God save the Queen!

Long live the King!

Heaven be praised!

b) *The subjunctive in subordinate clauses*

i) In clauses of condition the past subjunctive is very common; see 13a) ii above. The present subjunctive is highly formal or literary:

if this be true, old hopes are born anew

except in the common set expression **if need be** (= if necessary):

if need be, we can sell the furniture

Note also the concessive use:

they are all interrogated, be they friend or foe

ii) Clauses of comparison, introduced by **as if** or **as though** often, but by no means regularly, contain a past subjunctive:

he looks as though he took his work seriously (= ... as though he takes ...)

he treats me as if I was/were a child

iii) The past subjunctive is used after **if only** and in object clauses after **wish** and **had rather**, all such clauses expressing wish or desire:

if only we had a bigger house, life would be perfect

are you going abroad this year? – I wish I were/was

I wish he was/were back at school

where's your passport? – I wish I knew

do you want me to tell you? – I'd rather you didn't

iv) In formal language (eg legal language) the present subjunctive is sometimes found in object clauses after verbs or impersonal phrases (such as **it is desirable/it is important**) that express suggestion or wish:

we propose that the clause be extended to cover such eventualities

it is important that he take steps immediately

it is imperative that this matter be discussed further

In such clauses, the subjunctive is commoner in American than in British English, and is by no means infrequent outside the language of negotiation or legal language. Although American is rapidly influencing British English in this respect, the latter still prefers **should** + infinitive:

we suggest that the system (should) be changed

I am adamant that this (should) be put to the vote

it is vital that he (should) start as soon as possible

v) After **it's time**, when the speaker wishes to emphasize that something **ought** to be done, the past subjunctive is used:

it's time we spoke to him

it's high time they stopped that

whereas in the following example all that is expressed is the suitability of the time:

it's time to speak to him about it

vi) **if I was/if I were:**

There is often confusion about the correctness of **if I was/if I were**.

There are cases when only **if I was** is possible. This is when the condition referred to is in no sense an unreal condition, for example:

if I was mistaken about it then it certainly wasn't through lack of trying

The speaker is not questioning the reality of the mistake, but only explaining the cause.

On the other hand in the sentence:

if I were mistaken about it, surely I would have realized

the speaker is bringing the reality of the mistake into some doubt and so use of the subjunctive **were** is appropriate. But **was** would not be wrong in this context either — it is simply a more colloquial style.

15   THE ATTITUDINAL PAST TENSE

We have seen in 13 and 14 how the past subjunctive can refer to present time in conditional (and other) clauses. Apart from such uses of the past subjunctive, the past tense can refer to present time in main clauses that express a tentative, and therefore often more polite and deferential, attitude. Thus:

did you want to see me?

is more polite or tentative or less abrupt than:

do you want to see me?

But in the usage:

I was wondering if you could help me with this

the past tense has become fixed as a polite means of expression and is little or no different from:

I wonder if you could help me with this

The usage:

I was hoping you could help me with this

as a form of polite request, does not have a corresponding present tense construction.

16 THE PASSIVE

For the difference in form and basic meaning between active and passive, see p 139.

a) *The direct and the indirect passive*

In the active sentence:

they sent him another bill

another bill is the direct object and **him** the indirect object. If, in a corresponding passive construction, the active direct object becomes the passive subject, we have a 'direct passive':

another bill was sent (to) him

whereas an 'indirect passive' would have as its subject the indirect object of the active:

he was sent another bill

b) *The stative and the dynamic passive*

In the following sentence the verb expresses a state:

the shop is closed

whereas in the following example, there is no doubt that it expresses an action:

the shop is closed by his mother at 4 pm every day

In the first sentence the verb is said to be 'stative', in the second 'dynamic'. We know this from the context, not from the form, unlike many other languages which would have separate stative and dynamic passives, eg German and the Scandinavian languages. The lack of distinctions of form in English may occasionally lead to ambiguous sentences like:

his neck was broken when they lifted him

meaning either (stative) 'his neck had (already) been broken when they lifted him' or (dynamic) 'his neck was broken as they lifted him'. Sometimes, if we wish to stress the (often more dramatic) dynamic aspect, **get** can be used as the auxiliary instead of **be**, especially in non-formal language:

his neck got broken when they lifted him

they finally got caught

he got kicked out of the pub

It is also possible to use the verb **have** to indicate a dynamic passive:

he had his neck broken when they lifted him

they've had their house burgled three times

c) *Passive versus active*

   i) If the 'doer' of an action is less important than the thing done, the passive is often preferred to the active. Thus in:

   his invitation was refused

   the speaker evidently considers the identity of the 'refuser(s)' irrelevant. The reason why scientific language in particular contains an unusually high number of passives is precisely that mentioning the agent or 'doer' of scientific experimentation is felt to be too personal, not sufficiently objective, since the focus is then not solely on the experiment but also on the experimenter. Science freshmen at universities soon learn to write:

   the experiment was conducted in darkness

   rather than

   I conducted the experiment in darkness

   ii) If the 'doer' is completely irrelevant or not known at all, many verbs appear in the active with passive meaning. There is little difference between:

   the theatre runs at a profit

   and

   the theatre is run at a profit

or between:

her eyes were filled with tears (dynamic sense)

and

her eyes filled with tears

Such active forms with passive meaning are relatively common in English; and often a passive form would even be awkward or impossible:

the air felt warm

silk blouses do not wash well

this essay reads better than your last one

it flies beautifully (eg said by a pilot of a plane he is flying)

where is the film showing?

he photographs well

This last example does not mean that he takes good pictures; it means that he looks good in them.

iii) Sometimes the active form with passive meaning is confined to the infinitive:

the house is to let

I am to blame

the truth is not to seek here (or **... be sought ...** - this is literary usage)

but such instances are rare. However, in constructions like **there is** + (pro)noun with infinitive, the active infinitive with passive meaning is common:

there is work to do (= ... to be done)

when we get home there'll be suitcases to unpack

there was plenty to eat

there are still a lot of repairs to make

have you got anything to wash?

have you got anything to mend?

In some instances active and passive infinitive are interchangeable (in the last two examples, for instance):

there's nothing else to say/to be said

is there anything to gain/to be gained from it?

But sometimes after the pronouns **something**, **anything**, **nothing** in such constructions there can be a difference between the active infinitive (with passive meaning) and the passive infinitive of **do**. For example:

there is always something to do

would normally (but not necessarily) mean 'there's always something that will keep us occupied or entertained', whereas:

there is always something to be done

would mean 'there's always work that needs to be done'.

17 BE, HAVE, DO

a) *be*

i) **Be** is used as an auxiliary together with the past participle to form the passive and together with the present participle for the continuous aspect of the passive (p 139). Occasionally **be** can replace **have** as an auxiliary for the perfective aspect (p 139), as in:

are you finished?

our happiness is gone

In such instances there is particular emphasis on the present state rather than the action.

ii) Like the modal auxiliaries, **be** does not take **do** in negations and questions. However, when **be** functions as an independent verb rather than an auxiliary, **do** is used in negative imperatives:

don't be silly

iii) When **be** is an independent verb (ie not an auxiliary), it is not used in the continuous aspect, except when it refers exclusively to behaviour. Thus there is a difference between:

he is silly (= by nature)

and

he is being silly (= he is acting or behaving in a silly way)

and between:

he's American

and

if you said it that way, I'd assume you were deliberately being American

b) *have*

i) **Have** is used with the past participle to form the perfective aspect (p 138).

As an independent verb it sometimes indicates activity or experience, as in:

have dinner	**have difficulty**
have a chat	**have a good time**

When **have** does not indicate activity, it normally refers to possession, state or arrangement, as in:

have a farm	**have an appointment**
have toothache	**have time (for** or **to do something)**

So:

she'll have the baby in August

belongs to the first type if it means that she'll give birth to the baby. If, on the other hand, it means that she'll receive the baby, it belongs to the second type.

The types can be called **have 1** (+ **activity**) and **have 2** (− **activity**).

ii) *have 1*:

* This behaves like normal independent verbs in
  questions and negations, ie it takes **do**, also in tag-
  questions:

  did you have the day off yesterday?

  we don't have conversations any more

  we had a marvellous time, didn't we?

* Have 1 can be used in the continuous aspect:

  he telephoned as we were having lunch

  I'm having trouble with Carol these days

iii) *have 2*:

* Instead of **have 2** we often use **have got** in British
  English, especially in informal language, and mostly in
  the present tense:

  he has/he has got/he's got a large garden

  In the past tense we normally use **had** or **used to have**,
  the latter emphasizing prolonged possession, repetition
  or habit:

  they all had flu in July last year

  he had/used to have a large garden once

  we had/used to have lots of problems in those days

* In questions the subject and **have** may be inverted:

  have you any other illnesses?

  In negations **not** may be used without **do**:

  he hasn't a garden

  Such sentences are sometimes considered rather
  formal, everyday language preferring either **have ...
  got** or a **do**-construction:

  have you got/do you have any other illnesses?

  he hasn't got/doesn't have a garden

The **do**-version has been receiving a recent boost from American English, where it is normal. It should be noted that if the speaker wants to convey habitual, regular or general occurrence, then the **do**-version is particularly frequent:

have you got/do you have any nuts for those birds?

but:

do you always have nuts on the sideboard?

where **have** is very similar to 'keep' in meaning.

Similarly:

have you got/do you have a pain in your chest?

but:

do you frequently have a pain in your chest?

In tag-questions after **have**, both **have** and **do** are possible since, as we have seen, **have** can be used with or without **do** in full questions. **Do**, on the increase because of American usage, is particularly common in the past tense:

he has a Rolls, hasn't/doesn't he?

they had a large garden once, didn't they/hadn't they?

But after **have got** only **have** is possible in the tag-question:

he's got a Rolls, hasn't he?

Note the following difference between British and American English:

have you a minute? – no, I haven't (British)

have you a minute? – no, I don't (American)

* The continuous aspect is not possible with **have 2** unless it refers to the future. Thus:

they are having a fridge

cannot mean 'they possess a fridge'; it means 'in the

future they will possess a fridge'. In:

today I'm having the car

am having = 'am taking/using', which is a **have 1** type of meaning.

iv) The causative use of **have**:

The verb **have** is used in constructions of the form **have something done** in order to express the idea that the subject of the sentence is not directly responsible for the action expressed by the verb, but that he/she 'causes' someone else to do this action. For example:

they're having a new porch built

could you have these photocopied?

I'll have it done immediately

we'll have to have the loo fixed

what on earth have you had done to your hair!

Note that **get** can be substituted for **have** in all but the last of these examples.

* In one American usage the implication that someone else carries out the action has been largely lost:

Mr Braithwaite is here — ah, have him come in

This is simply equivalent to a request to ask Mr Braithwaite to come in.

v) Passive constructions:

The verb **have** also has a use in forming a type of passive construction, particularly when the implication is that the subject of the sentence has suffered in some way (see also 16 b):

he's had all his money stolen

he's had two wives killed in car crashes

c) *do*

The use of **do** in questions and negations has been dealt with – see p 156 – 158. For its use in other cases of inversion (eg **never once did I dream he would!**) see p 243.

i) Emphatic **do**:

In sentences that are neither questions nor negations a stressed **do** before the main verb can be used for emphasis:

oh, I do like your new jacket!

do try to keep still!

he doesn't know any German but he does know a little French

I didn't manage to get tickets for . . . but I did get some for . . .

And the verb **do** itself can be used with **do** as an emphatic auxiliary:

well, if you don't do that, what do you do?

we don't do much skiing, but what we do do is go hill-walking

ii) **do** as verb replacement:

Some examples of this have been given under tag-questions (see p 157). Other examples are:

she never drinks! – oh yes, she does

can I help myself to another cream cake? – please do

do you both agree? – I do, but she doesn't

18 THE MODAL AUXILIARIES

These are **will-would, shall-should, can-could, may-might, must-had to, ought to.**

a) *will-would*

The contracted negative forms are **won't-wouldn't.**

i) For conditional sentences, see p 170.

ii) To express future time: for a general survey, see p 165.

iii) To express commands rather than pure future:

you will do as you are told!

new recruits will report to headquarters on Tuesday at 8.30 am

will you stop that right now!

iv) To appeal, rather formally, to somebody's memory or knowledge:

you will recall last week's discussion about the purchase of a computer

you will all know that the inspector has completed his report

v) To express assumption rather than the future:

there's the telephone, Mary! — oh, that will be John (= I assume that it is John who is ringing)

they'll be there by now

how old is he now? — he'll be about 45

vi) To emphasize natural, inherent ability, capacity, inclination or characteristic behaviour rather than the future:

cork will float on water (= cork floats on water)

the Arts Centre will hold about 300 people (= ... holds about 300 people)

John will sit playing with a matchbox for hours

on cold winter nights they will cuddle up to each other and watch TV in bed

boys will be boys

it's so annoying, he will keep interrupting! (stress on 'will' when spoken)

the car won't start

well, if you will drive so fast, what do you expect?

Similarly **would**, to refer to the past:

when he was little, John would sit playing with a matchbox for hours

she created a scene in public — she would! (= how typical of her)

vii) Asking questions, offering:

will you have another cup?

won't you try some of these?

viii) Making requests:

will you move your car, please?

A slightly more polite request is:

would you move your car, please?

ix) Expressing determination:

I will not stand for this!

I will be obeyed!

b) *shall-should*

The contracted negative forms are **shan't-shouldn't**.

i) For conditional sentences, see p 170.

ii) For the equivalent of a subjunctive, see p 173.

iii) To express future time, see p 165.

iv) (**shall** only) In legal or official language **shall** is often used to express an obligation. This meaning of **shall** is very similar to 'must':

the committee shall consist of no more than six members

the contract shall be subject to English law

v) (**should** only) obligation (often moral obligation):

you should lose some weight

he should try to save his marriage

he shouldn't be allowed to

you really should see this film

is everything as it should be?

something was not quite as it should be

vi) (**should** only) deduction, probability:

it's ten o'clock, they should be back any minute

John should have finished putting up those shelves by now

are they there? — I don't know, but they should be

vii) (**should** only) tentative statements:

I should just like to say that . . .

I should hardly think that's right

will he agree? — I shouldn't think so

viii) **Should** is often used to refer to the **idea** (as opposed to the **fact**) of an action. This use of **should** is sometimes referred to as 'putative':

that she should want to take early retirement is quite understandable

Compare this with:

it is quite understandable that she wanted to take early retirement

The difference is subtle. In the first example the

emphasis is shifted to the idea that she wanted to take early retirement; in the second the emphasis is shifted to the fact that she did.

It is important to note that this **should** is neutral as far as time reference is concerned. The first example above may equally well refer to the past (she has taken early retirement) or to the future (she will be taking early retirement) according to the context. The second example, of course, can only refer to the past.

The putative use of **should** can be compared with **should** after verbs or impersonal constructions of suggestion, wish or command, discussed in the section on the subjunctive, p 173.

In the above example putative **should** occurred in a subordinate clause, but it may also appear in main clauses:

where have I put my glasses? – how should I know?
(= how can you possibly imagine that I might know?)

as we were sitting there, who should walk by but Joan Collins! (= just imagine who walked by!)

there was a knock at the door, and who should it be but . . .

c) *can-could*

The contracted negative forms are **can't-couldn't**. The non-contracted present negative is **cannot**.

i) ability (= be able to):

I can swim

when I was young, I could swim for hours

The second sentence refers to past ability. However, in conditional clauses **could** + simple infinitive refers to the present or future (compare **would** under **Expressing Condition**, p 170):

if you try/tried harder, you could lose weight

ii) permission:

can/could I have a sweet?

Note that **could** refers as much to the present or future as **can**. The only difference is that **could** is a little more tentative or polite. All the same, **could** may sometimes be used for past permission when the context is clearly past:

for some reason we couldn't smoke in the lounge yesterday; but today we can

There is often a slight difference between **can** and **may** in the sense of 'being allowed' in that, normally, **can** is less formal than **may**.

iii) possibility:

what shall we do tonight? — well, we can/could watch a film

Again we note that **could** does not refer to the past but to the present or future. If the reference to the past has to be made, **could** must be followed by the infinitive perfect:

instead of going to the pub we could have watched a film

I could have (could've) gone there if I'd wanted to, but I didn't

There is sometimes an important difference between **can** and **may** in their reference to possibility: **can** frequently expresses straightforward logical possibility whereas **may** often implies uncertainty, chance or a certain degree of likelihood of something happening:

(a) **your comments can be overheard**

(b) **your comments may be overheard**

(a) says that it is possible to overhear the comments (eg because they are very loud) whether or not it is likely that anybody actually will.

(b) says that there is some likelihood that the comments actually will be overheard.

This difference is also seen in negative clauses:

he can't have heard us (= it is impossible for him to have heard us)

he may not have heard us (= it is possible that he did not hear us)

iv) (**could** only) suggestions:

you could be a little kinder

he could express himself more clearly

This is sometimes used with an element of reproach:

you could have let us know!

he could have warned us!

d) *may-might*

The contracted negative **mayn't** is gradually disappearing in the 'permission' use of **may**; instead **may not** or **must not/mustn't** or **can't** are used to express negative permission, ie prohibition. The contracted negative of **might** is **mightn't** but this is not used in the 'permission' sense.

i) permission:

you may sit down (compare **can** in c) ii above)

may I open a window? – no, you may not!

you must not/mustn't open the windows in here

A speaker who uses **might** to express permission is distinctly polite:

I wonder if I might have another wee glass of sherry

might I suggest we adjourn the meeting?

Note that **might** refers to the present or future. It very rarely refers to the past when used in a main clause.

Compare:

he then asked if he might smoke (rather formal)

he then asked if he was allowed to smoke

and

he wasn't allowed to smoke

Might is not possible in the last example. Only in special cases can **might** be used to refer to the past in main clauses:

in those days we were told not to drink; nor might we smoke or be out after 10 o'clock

A more usual, less literary, way of putting this sentence would be:

in those days we were told not to drink; nor were we allowed to smoke or be out after 10 o'clock

ii) possibility:

it may/might rain

they may/might be right

it mayn't/mightn't be so easy as you think

he may/might have left already

Might normally expresses a lesser degree of possibility.

Note the idiomatic use:

and who may/might you be?

in which use of **may/might** introduces a note of surprise or amusement or, perhaps, annoyance into the question:

and who *may/might* he be to give out orders?

iii) Note the use of **might** to make suggestions:

you might help me dry the dishes

well, you might at least try!

you might have a look at chapter 2 for next Wednesday

he might be a little less abrupt

they might at least apologize

This usage often implies a sense of reproach:

you might have warned us what would happen!

he might have tried to stop it!

iv) wishes:

may the best man win!

may you be forgiven for telling such lies!

might I be struck dumb if I tell a lie!

This usage is normally confined to fixed expressions (as in the first example) or is considered somewhat rhetorical or literary (as in the other two).

e) *must-had to*

i) obligation:

you must try harder

we must park the car here and walk the rest of the way

Note that **had to** is used for the past. **Must** can only be used for the past in indirect speech, and even in such cases **had to** is more common:

you said the other day that you had to/must clean out the garden shed

It is also possible to use **have to**, or the less formal **have got to**, in the present tense. The difference between **must** and **have (got) to** is normally one of personal feelings of obligation or compulsion (**must**) versus external obligation (**have (got) to**). Compare:

I must go and visit my friend in hospital (= I feel it's necessary to go)

you must go and visit your friend in hospital (= I feel it's necessary that you go . . .)

I have (got) to be at the hospital by 4 pm (ie the hospital has arranged for me to be there at 4 pm)

ii) negatives:

The negatives require special care. **Must not/mustn't** can be used but only to express prohibition (= an obligation not to do something):

we mustn't park the car here (= we're not allowed to park here)

you mustn't take so many pills (= do not take so many pills)

But if the negative obligation means not that it is, for example, forbidden to do something, but that there is no need or obligation to do something, then **don't have to** or **haven't got to** must be used:

we don't have to park here, we could always drive a little further

you don't have to take so many pills (= you needn't take ...)

we haven't got to be there before 9 (= it's not necessary to arrive before 9)

iii) deduction, probability:

if they're over 65, they must be old age pensioners

you must be joking!

they must have been surprised to see you

Have to is often used in this sense:

you have to be kidding!

and so is **have got to**, especially in British English:

well if she said so, it's got to be true (it's = it has)

For the negative use **can**:

he can't be that old!

f) *ought to*

The contracted negative is **oughtn't to**, and the infinitive after **ought** has **to** in contrast to other modal auxiliaries.

i) obligation:

Ought to is similar in meaning to **should** in its sense of obligation:

you oughtn't to speak to her like that

I ought to be going now

I know I really ought (to), but I don't want to

ii) deduction, probability:

they ought to have reached the summit by now

20 square metres? – that ought to be enough

Compare this difference between **ought to** and **must**:

if they possess all these things, they must be rich (logical deduction)

if they possess all these things, they ought to be happy (logical expectation or probability – or moral obligation)

g) *used to*

Since it is possible to form questions and negative sentences containing **used to** without **do**, some people consider **used to** a kind of semi-auxiliary. The use of **do** is, however, at least equally common:

he used not/usedn't to visit us so often

he didn't use to visit us so often

In questions the form without **do** is less common, more written than spoken style:

used you to live abroad?

did you use to live abroad?

Often **never** is used instead of **not**:

> **he never used to visit us so often**

Used to expresses habitual action in the past but without the strong sense of typical or characteristic behaviour that **would** conveys (see a) vi above):

> **John used to play badminton when he was younger**
>
> **I used to live abroad**
>
> **do you smoke? — I used to**

19 DARE, NEED

These verbs can behave as either ordinary verbs or as modal auxiliaries. When they are auxiliaries, they take no **-s** in the 3rd person singular present tense; **do** is not used in questions and negations; and a following infinitive is without **to**.

a) *As ordinary verbs*

> **he didn't dare to speak**
>
> **does he really dare to talk openly about it?**
>
> **I dare you** (= I challenge you)
>
> **he needs some money**
>
> **you don't need to pay for them now**
>
> **all he needs to do now is buy the tickets**

However, **dare** may be half an ordinary verb (eg with **do** in questions and negations) and half an auxiliary (followed by an infinitive without **to**):

> **does he really dare talk openly about it?**

but the infinitive with **to** must be used after the present participle:

> **not daring to speak to her, he quietly left the room**

In affirmative **main** clauses (ie main clauses that are not questions or negations) **need** can only be an ordinary verb:

> **the child needs to go to the toilet**

b) *As modal auxiliaries*

> **he dared not speak**
>
> **dare he talk openly about it?**
>
> **this is as much as I dare spend on it**
>
> **you needn't pay for them right now**
>
> **need we take the dog?**
>
> **all he need do now is buy the tickets**

Note **I dare say** = 'probably':

> **I dare say he's going to fail**
>
> **is it going to rain, do you think? − I dare say it will**

20 PREPOSITIONAL VERBS AND PHRASAL VERBS

a) *Prepositional verbs*

i) It is important to distinguish between a 'verb + prepositional phrase' ((a) and (c) below) and a 'prepositional verb + object' ((b) and (d)). In the latter case the preposition functions as a **particle** belonging to the verb, ie as a verb-extension. Compare the two sentences:

(a) **they danced after dinner**

(b) **they looked after the child**

Superficially those two sentences look as if they have the same structure, and yet when we take a closer look, we feel that the two words **look after** form a single verb unit (compare 'they nursed the child'), whereas **danced after** do not: **after dinner** is a prepositional phrase detached from the verb and functioning as an adverbial of time in (a), whereas **the child** is the direct object of **look after** in (b). The same difference can be observed in eg:

(c) **they went through Germany**

(d) **they went through the accounts** (= examined)

ii) **Look after** and **go through** (= examine (or suffer)) are prepositional verbs. These are often highly idiomatic, ie their sense cannot be deduced from the individual parts, which rarely have a literal meaning. Some other examples are:

go by (= follow (instructions))

pick on (= treat in an overcritical manner)

get at (= treat unkindly; bribe)

you can't do your own thing; you have to go by the book

the teacher's always picking on him

my mother is always getting at me

I'm sure the jury have been got at

iii) Certain structures that would be possible with 'verb + prepositional phrase' are impossible with prepositional verbs. For instance, questions with prepositional verbs allow the use of the pronouns **who** and **what**, but not the adverbs **where, when, how**:

they looked after the girl/who(m) did they look after?

they went through the accounts/what did they go through?

the police officer grappled with the thug/who(m) did he grapple with?

But it does not make sense to ask **where did they look?/where did they go?/how** (or **where**) **did he grapple?** On the other hand 'verb + prepositional phrase' will often allow adverb questions:

they went through Germany/where did they go?

they worked with great care/how did they work?

they danced after dinner/when did they dance?

iv) Because a prepositional verb is felt to be one single unit, it can often (but not always) be used in the passive:

the child has been looked after very well indeed

the accounts have been gone through

do you feel you're being got at?

The passive cannot be used with 'verb + prepositional phrase'. We can't say **the dinner was danced after** or **great care has been worked with**.

b) *Phrasal verbs*

i) One important difference between phrasal verbs and prepositional verbs is the possibility for phrasal verbs of allowing an object to precede the particle:

look up these words/look these words up

turn down the television/turn the television down

have you switched on the computer?/have you switched the computer on?

have you tried on any of their new line of shoes?/have you tried any of their new line of shoes on?

And if the object is a pronoun, the particle **must** follow it:

look them up/turn it down/switch it on

ii) Whereas prepositional verbs are always transitive (when seen as a complete unit), some phrasal verbs are always intransitive, some are always transitive, and some can be either:

back up (= support − transitive only):

he always backs her up

lose out (= be at a disadvantage − intransitive only):

poor people often lose out

cool down (= make less warm — transitive):

cool the rolls down in the fridge

cool down (= become less warm — intransitive):

let the rolls cool down

iii) Phrasal verbs do not allow the particle-preposition to precede a relative pronoun; prepositional verbs do. Thus we can say:

this is a man on whom you can rely

because **rely on** is a prepositional verb, whereas it is impossible to say:

this is his wife up whom he has always backed

since **back up** is a phrasal verb.

iv) Like a great number of prepositional verbs (see a)ii above) many phrasal verbs are very idiomatic:

live down (= forget — a bad incident)
square up (= settle — debts etc)
bring round (= revive — unconscious person; persuade)
set back (= to cost — somebody money):

that court case has affected her; she'll never be able to live it down

if you pay now, we can square up later

give him a brandy; that'll bring him round

do you think anything will bring him round to our point of view?

that car must have set you back at least £10,000

c) *Phrasal-prepositional verbs*

These are, like prepositional verbs, always transitive and consist of not two but three words, eg:

look forward to

They do not allow the object to come between the verb and its particles, ie we cannot say things like **have you been looking it forward to?** The object has to come after the last particle:

we've been looking forward to it

Nor do these verbs allow both particles to precede a relative pronoun. Thus we would say:

is there anything else (which) we can look forward to?

or:

is there anything else to which we can look forward?

but it is NOT possible to put both particles before a relative as in **is there anything else forward to which we can look?**

Other examples of (idiomatic) phrasal-prepositional verbs:

make off with (= steal)

make up to (= try to gain the favour of)

live up to (= behave according to a high standard)

stand up for (= support − in a dispute)

crack down on (= treat severely)

somebody made off with her suitcase

this is the teacher Fiona has been making up to throughout term, but her marks are no better

he had aquired a reputation which was difficult to live up to

why didn't you stand up for me if you knew I was right?

every Christmas police crack down on drink-and-drive offenders

21 TENSE IN INDIRECT SPEECH

Indirect speech is a **report** of what somebody has said:

direct speech: **Henry said, 'I am unhappy'**

indirect speech: **Henry said that he was unhappy**

Tenses in direct and indirect speech sometimes coincide, and sometimes they don't.

a) *Tense change*

There is a change of tense if the verb of utterance is in the past tense (simple or perfective):

i) The present tense of direct speech is changed to the past tense in indirect speech:

Henry said/had said, 'I am unhappy' (direct)

Henry said/had said (that) he was unhappy (indirect)

This also applies to the modal auxiliaries:

Henry said/had said, 'I can do it' (direct)

Henry said/had said (that) he could do it (indirect)

Henry said/had said, 'She will regret that' (direct)

Henry said/had said (that) she would regret that (indirect)

* Note that **shall** after I and we is changed to **would** (not **should**) in indirect speech:

Henry said/had said, 'I/we shall be in Rome next year' (direct)

Henry said/had said (that) he/they would be in Rome next year (indirect)

ii) Both the past tense and the present perfect of direct speech are changed to the past perfect in indirect speech:

Henry said/had said, 'I was unhappy' (direct)

Henry said/had said (that) he had been unhappy (indirect)

Henry said/had said, 'I have been unhappy' (direct)

Henry said/had said (that) he had been unhappy (indirect)

Exceptions:

* If the truth or validity of a statement that was made in the past applies equally to the present, a tense change is not necessary (although it may be made):

Pope said that the proper study of mankind is (was) man

* Nor is a tense change necessary if the indirect speech occurs at a time very close to that of the original direct speech:

'I was ill last week' (direct)

John just said (that) he was ill last week (indirect)

b) *No tense change*

See also a) ii exceptions above.

i) There is no change of tense if the verb reporting what is/was said is in the present (simple or perfective):

Henry says/has said, 'I am unhappy' (direct)

Henry says/has said (that) he is unhappy (indirect)

Henry says/has said, 'I was unhappy' (direct)

Henry says/has said (that) he was unhappy (indirect)

ii) If the direct speech contains a past perfect, this remains in the indirect speech:

'we had already met Olga by that time' (direct)

we insist(ed) (that) we had already met Olga by that time (indirect)

iii) If the past tense of the direct speech refers to the present or future as in conditional sentences (see 13 a)iii above) then there is no tense change:

'if you saw her, you wouldn't recognize her' (direct)

he says/said that if you saw her, you wouldn't recognize her (indirect)

c) *The auxiliaries must and should*

i) **Must** is not used in the past tense (which is normally **had to**) except in indirect speech:

he had told them that they must be prepared

But even in such cases **had to** is very common:

he had told them that they had to be prepared

ii) **Should** after **I** and **we** in direct-speech conditional sentences (see 13a) ii and b) i above) changes to **would** in indirect speech:

'if I won that amount of money, I should just spend it all' (direct)

he says/said (that) if he won that amount of money, he would just spend it all (indirect)

But **should** meaning 'ought to' does not change:

'we should go and visit mother in hospital' (direct)

Jean says/said (that) we should go and visit mother in hospital (indirect)

22 LIST OF IRREGULAR VERBS

American forms have been indicated by *. Unusual, archaic or literary forms are given in brackets.

infinitive	*past simple*	*past participle*
abide	(abode) [1]	abided
arise	arose	arisen
awake	awoke, awaked	awoken, (awaked)
bear	bore	borne [2]
beat	beat	beaten [3]
become	became	become
befall	befell	befallen
beget	begot	begotten
begin	began	begun
behold	beheld	beheld
bend	bent	bent [4]
bereave	bereaved	bereft [5]
beseech	besought	besought
bestride	bestrode	bestridden
bet	bet, betted	bet, betted
bid (*offer*)	bid	bid
bid (*command*)	bade	bidden
bind	bound	bound
bite	bit	bitten
bleed	bled	bled
blow	blew	blown
break	broke	broken [6]
breed	bred	bred
bring	brought	brought
broadcast	broadcast	broadcast
build	built	built
burn	burnt, burned	burnt, burned
burst	burst	burst
buy	bought	bought
cast	cast	cast
catch	caught	caught
chide	chid, chided	chid, (chidden), chided

choose	chose	chosen
cleave (*cut*)	clove, cleft,	cloven, cleft [7]
cleave (*adhere*)	cleaved, (clave)	cleaved
cling	clung	clung
clothe	clothed, (clad)	clothed, (clad)
come	came	come
cost	cost	cost
creep	crept	crept
crow	crowed, (crew)	crowed
cut	cut	cut
dare	dared, (durst)	dared, (durst)
deal	dealt	dealt
dig	dug	dug
dive	dived, dove*	dived
draw	drew	drawn
dream	dreamt, dreamed	dreamt, dreamed
drink	drank	drunk [8]
drive	drove	driven
dwell	dwelt, dwelled	dwelt, dwelled
eat	ate	eaten
fall	fell	fallen
feed	fed	fed
feel	felt	felt
fight	fought	fought
find	found	found
fit	fit*, fitted	fit*, fitted
flee	fled	fled
fling	flung	flung
fly	flew	flown
forbear	forbore	forborne
forbid	forbad(e)	forbidden
forget	forgot	forgotten
forgive	forgave	forgiven
forsake	forsook	forsaken
freeze	froze	frozen
get	got	got, gotten* [9]
gild	gilt, gilded	gilt, gilded [10]
gird	girt, girded	girt, girded [10]
give	gave	given
go	went	gone

grind	ground	ground
grow	grew	grown
hang	hung, hanged [11]	hung, hanged [11]
hear	heard	heard
heave	hove, heaved [12]	hove, heaved [12]
hew	hewed	hewn, hewed
hide	hid	hidden
hit	hit	hit
hold	held	held
hurt	hurt	hurt
keep	kept	kept
kneel	knelt, kneeled	knelt, kneeled
knit	knit, knitted [13]	knit, knitted [13]
know	knew	known
lay	laid	laid
lead	led	led
lean	leant, leaned	leant, leaned
leap	leapt, leaped	leapt, leaped
learn	learnt, learned	learnt, learned
leave	left	left
lend	lent	lent
let	let	let
lie	lay	lain
light	lit, lighted	lit, lighted [14]
lose	lost	lost
make	made	made
mean	meant	meant
meet	met	met
melt	melted	melted, molten [15]
mow	mowed	mown, mowed
pay	paid	paid
plead	pled*, pleaded	pled*, pleaded [16]
put	put	put
quit	quit, (quitted)	quit, (quitted) [17]
read	read	read
rend	rent	rent
rid	rid, (ridded)	rid
ride	rode	ridden
ring	rang	rung
rise	rose	risen

run	ran	run
saw	sawed	sawn, sawed
say	said	said
see	saw	seen
seek	sought	sought
sell	sold	sold
send	sent	sent
set	set	set
sew	sewed	sewn, sewed
shake	shook	shaken
shear	sheared	shorn, sheared [18]
shed	shed	shed
shine	shone [19]	shone [19]
shoe	shod, shoed	shod, shoed [20]
shoot	shot	shot
show	showed	shown, showed
shrink	shrank, shrunk	shrunk, shrunken [21]
shut	shut	shut
sing	sang	sung
sink	sank	sunk, sunken [22]
sit	sat	sat
slay	slew	slain
sleep	slept	slept
slide	slid	slid
sling	slung	slung
slink	slunk	slunk
slit	slit	slit
smell	smelt, smelled	smelt, smelled
smite	smote	smitten
sneak	snuck*, sneaked	snuck*, sneaked
sow	sowed	sown, sowed
speak	spoke	spoken
speed	sped, speeded	sped, speeded
spell	spelt, spelled	spelt, spelled
spend	spent	spent
spill	spilt, spilled	spilt, spilled
spin	spun	spun
spit	spat, spit*	spat, spit*

split	split	split
spoil	spoilt, spoiled	spoilt, spoiled
spread	spread	spread
spring	sprang	sprung
stand	stood	stood
steal	stole	stolen
stick	stuck	stuck
sting	stung	stung
stink	stank	stunk
strew	strewed	strewn, strewed
stride	strode	stridden
strike	struck	struck, stricken [23]
string	strung	strung
strive	strove	striven
swear	swore	sworn
sweat	sweat*, sweated	sweat*, sweated
sweep	swept	swept
swell	swelled	swollen, swelled [24]
swim	swam	swum
swing	swung	swung
take	took	taken
teach	taught	taught
tear	tore	torn
tell	told	told
think	thought	thought
thrive	thrived, (throve)	thrived, (thriven)
throw	threw	thrown
thrust	thrust	thrust
tread	trod	trodden
understand	understood	understood
undertake	undertook	undertaken
wake	woke, waked	woken, waked
wear	wore	worn
weave	wove [25]	woven [25]
weep	wept	wept
wet	wet*, wetted [26]	wet*, wetted [26]
win	won	won
wind	wound	wound
wring	wrung	wrung
write	wrote	written

(1) Regular in the combination **abide by** 'obey': **they abided by the rules**.

(2) But **born** if in the passive = 'given birth to' or as an adjective: **he was born in France/a born gentleman**.

(3) Note the colloquial **this has me beat/you have me beat there** and **beat** in the sense of very tired: **I am (dead) beat**.

(4) Note the phrase **on one's bended knees**.

(5) But **bereaved** if it implies loss by death, as in **the bereaved received no compensation**. Compare: **he was bereft of speech**.

(6) But **broke** as an adjective = without money: **I'm broke**.

(7) **Cleft** can only be used in the sense 'to cut in two'. Note **cleft palate** and **(to be caught) in a cleft stick**, but **cloven foot/hoof**.

(8) As an adjective before a noun **drunken** 'intoxicated, given to drink' is sometimes used (**a lot of drunk(en) people**) and **must** be used before inanimate nouns (**one of his usual drunken parties**).

(9) But **have got to** also in American when it means 'must': **a man has got to do what a man has got to do**. Compare: **she has gotten into a terrible mess**.

(10) Past participle **gilt** and **girt** are particularly common as adjectives before nouns: **gilt mirrors, a flower-girt grave** (but always **gilded youth**, where **gilded** means 'rich and fortunate').

(11) Regular in the sense 'execute by hanging'.

(12) **Hove** is nautical language whence the phrase **heave into sight**: **just then Mary hove into sight**.

(13) Irregular in the sense 'join closely' (**a close-knit family**), but normally regular in the sense 'make woollen garments' and when referring to bones.

(14) When the past participle is used as an adjective before a noun, **lighted** is often preferred to **lit: a lighted match** (but: **the match is lit, she has lit a match**). In compounds **lit** is used: **well-lit streets/the streets are well-lit.** In the figurative sense (with **up**) only **lit** is used in the past tense and past participle: **her face lit up when she saw me.**

(15) Only **molten** as an adjective before nouns, and only when it means 'melted at a very high temperature', eg **molten lead** (but **melted butter**).

(16) Past tense and past participle **pled** also in Scottish and American English.

(17) In American English the regular forms do not occur, and they are becoming increasingly rare in British English.

(18) The past participle is normally **shorn** before a noun (**newly-shorn lambs**) and always in the phrase **(to be) shorn of** '(to be) deprived of': **shorn of his riches he was nothing.**

(19) But regular in the sense 'polish' (American English).

(20) Only **shod** as an adjective: **a well-shod foot.**

(21) **Shrunken** is used only as an adjective: **shrunken limbs/her face was shrunken.**

(22) **Sunken** is used only as an adjective: **sunken eyes/her cheeks were sunken.**

(23) **Stricken** only in the figurative sense (**a stricken family/stricken with poverty**). It is particularly common in compounds: **poverty-stricken, fever-stricken, horror-stricken** (also **horror-struck**), **terror-stricken** (also **terror-struck**), but we always say **thunderstruck** 'very surprised'.

Also American usage as in 'the remark was stricken off the record'.

(24) **Swollen** is more common than **swelled** both as a verb (**her face has swollen**) and as an adjective (**her face is swollen/a swollen face**). A **swollen head** 'a high opinion of oneself' is a **swelled head** in American English.

(25) But regular when it means 'to move in and out': **the motorbike weaved elegantly through the traffic**.

(26) But irregular also in British English in the sense 'to wet with urine': **he wet his bed again last night**.

23 THE AUXILIARIES *BE*, *HAVE*, *DO*: FORMS

a) BE

Present	*Past*	*Past participle*
1st **I am**	1st **I was**	**been**
2nd **you are**	2nd **you were**	
3rd **he/she/it is**	3rd **he was**	
1st **we are**	1st **we were**	
2nd **you are**	2nd **you were**	
3rd **they are**	3rd **they were**	

Contracted with preceding word:

I'm = I am; you're = you are; he's/John's = he is/John is; we're/you're/they're = we are/you are/they are

Contracted with **not**:

aren't I? (questions only) = **am I not?**; **you/we/they aren't; he isn't; I/he wasn't; you/we/they weren't**

Also: **I'm not; you're not** etc.

For the subjunctive, see p 173.

b) **HAVE**

Present	*Past*	*Past Participle*
1st **I have**	1st **I had**	**had**
2nd **you have**	2nd **you had**	
3rd **he/she/it has**	3rd **he had**	
1st **we have**	1st **we had**	
2nd **you have**	2nd **you had**	
3rd **they have**	3rd **they had**	

Contracted with preceding word:

I've/you've/we've/they've = I have etc

he's = he has

I'd/you'd/he'd/we'd/they'd = I had etc

Note that **he's/she's** are not normally contracted when used in the present tense:

I've two cars

he has two cars

Contracted with **not**:

haven't; hasn't; hadn't

c) **DO**

Present	*Past*	*Past Participle*
1st **I do**	1st **I did**	**done**
2nd **you do**	2nd **you did**	
3rd **he/she/it does**	3rd **he did**	
1st **we do**	1st **we did**	
2nd **you do**	2nd **you did**	
3rd **they do**	3rd **they did**	

Contracted with **not**:

don't; doesn't; didn't

8. PREPOSITIONS

1   Prepositions express various relations, such as those of
time, place, possession etc, and are normally followed by
nouns or pronouns such as:

after — after the show

on — on the shelf

of — of London

Of course, in certain constructions English prepositions
can follow their (pro)noun:

the people I came here with

something I had never dreamed of

See also **Prepositional and Phrasal Verbs**, p 197, and
Interrogative and Relative Pronouns, p 113 and p 115.

Prepositional phrases have two main functions:

as noun modifiers:

the man from Rome has arrived

and as adverbials (of time, place etc):

the man arrived before the woman

the man arrived from Rome

2   The following is a list of the most important prepositions.
Since most prepositions have a wealth of meanings and
applications, only those uses that are important and also
particularly interesting or problematic for a learner of
English have been included.

★   **about** and **around**

i)   place: Often there is no difference between **about** and
around although American English prefers **around**:

they kept walking about/around the room

But **(a)round** often has a stronger connotation of '(part of) a circle' as in:

he lives just (a)round the corner

she put the rope (a)round his chest

ii) approximately:

I have about £1 on me

it'll cost you around £20

iii) concerning (only **about**):

what's the book about? – it's a story about love

Of has a similar meaning, but is more closely linked to the preceding noun (compare genitive **of**-phrases, p 52):

this is the story of my life

On is more technical, more academic:

he gave a paper on Verdi and Shakespeare

a book on English grammar

★ above

Above should be compared with **over**. There is frequently little to choose between them:

he has a lovely mirror above/over the mantelpiece

But **above** tends to be more precise as regards the vertical dimension than **over**:

clouds are hovering over the mountains

a few clouds are hovering just above the mountains

we're now about 2,000 feet above sea level

This is why things that are **above** other things don't touch them:

the shirts had been placed in the wardrobe above the socks and underwear

he flung his coat over a chair

★ **across**

Across and **over** are often very close in meaning, but **across** tends to be more precise about the horizontal dimension the way that **above** is about the vertical:

he walked across the fields to the farm

he laid out his suit diagonally across the bed

★ **after**

See also **behind** below.

i) In the figurative sense note the difference between **ask after** and **ask for**:

he asked after you (= he asked how you were)

he asked for you (= he asked to speak to you)

ii) in a figurative sense implying a goal:

they keep striving after the happiness which eludes them

iii) note also **after** = 'according to':

he's a man after my own heart

do it after the Parisian manner ('in' is more usual)

iv) In the temporal sense we may compare **after** and **since**. The difference between them relates to that between the past tense (**after**) and the present perfect (**since**). Compare:

he wasn't well after his journey

he hasn't been well since his journey

The same difference is still there without any verb forms. Thus there is a great difference between:

Britain after the war

and

Britain since the war

The first example refers more to the time immediately following the war, the second to the time up to the present from the completion of the war.

★ **against**

   i) This normally implies an obstacle of some kind:

      they didn't fight against them, they fought with them

      we're sailing against the current

   ii) But it may also simply imply contact after 'direction towards', as in:

      he knocked his head against the wall

   iii) denoting background:

      he held the picture against the wall

      he held the stone against/towards the light

★ **among(st)**

   Whereas **between** divides into two, **among(st)** does not:

   he sat between John and Joan

   he sat among(st) the flowers

   Note that 'dividing into two' does not necessarily mean that the two units are mentioned (as in the case of John and Joan above). It only means that a division into two separate people or things or groups or portions is implied. Thus it is perfectly correct to say:

   the road ran between the houses

   even if there were 250 of them. The point is that **between** is telling us that the road divides the houses into two groups. But, still referring to those 250 houses, we would say:

   the cats were running to and fro among the houses

   since now division into two groups is no longer the case. Of course, if there are only two houses, we would say:

   the cats were running to and fro between the houses

★ **at**

See also **to**.

At versus **in**: **at** refers to a point (often on some sort of scale, real or imagined). Thus we would say:

the big hand stopped at six o'clock

and

the train stops at Dundee, Edinburgh and York

since those cities are not regarded as cities in that sentence, but as stations on a route. But we would say:

he lives in Dundee

If I say that:

he is at Dundee

once again **Dundee** does not refer to the city; it refers to an institution, such as Dundee University.

With the verb **arrive**, **at** is also used for a 'point':

they finally arrived at their destination

otherwise **in**:

when we arrived in London, we went to look for a hotel

Figuratively, it is always **arrive at**:

have they arrived at any decision yet?

at versus **by**:

i) with expressions of place; compare:

(a) **he was sitting at the table**

(b) **he was sitting by the table**

At implies closeness to the point of contact; **by** just means 'very near'.

ii) with expressions of time; compare:

(a) **be there at six o'clock**

(b) **be there by six o'clock**

Once again **at** refers to a point (in time), whereas **by** means 'no later than'.

★ **before**

This refers to both time and space:

be there before six o'clock

he knelt before the Queen

i) In the spatial sense there is sometimes a difference between **before** and **in front of** in that the positional relationship often has subjective importance:

he was trembling before the judge

In front of is more literal with regards to position and is the word most often used in everyday English:

he was standing in front of the judge in the queue

Note also, in the last two examples, that **in front of** need not imply that the two are facing each other. **Before** does.

ii) With reference to time, the use of **before** with verbs in the negative can be usefully compared with **until**. **Before** means 'earlier in time than'; **until** means 'up to (a certain time)':

(a) **you will not get the letter before Monday**

(b) **you will not get the letter until Monday**

In (a) the letter will arrive on or after Monday (but not before); in (b) the letter will arrive on Monday.

* **behind**

    This sometimes gets close in meaning to **after**:

    (a) **he entered behind her**

    (b) **he entered after her**

    (c) **he shut the door behind/after him**

    Behind stresses 'at the back of', whereas **after** points to a sequence (since it also has a time sense). This difference is seen clearly in (a) and (b), but there is next to no difference between the two prepositions in (c).

* **below**

    Below corresponds to **above**, and **under** corresponds to **over**. See **above** above. Examples:

    we're now 50 metres below the snow-line

    he was sitting under the bridge

    below the bridge the water gets deeper

    his shoes were under the bed

* **beside** and **besides**

    beside = next to:

    sit beside me

    besides = in addition to, apart from:

    there were three guests there besides him and me

* **between** see **among**

* **beyond**

    When compared with other prepositions of place, **beyond** implies a relatively large distance. **Beyond** the church is further away than **on the other side of/above** or **below** the church.

    And, figuratively, something that is **beyond** me is **completely above** my head.

* **but**

> **But** as a preposition means 'except'. **Except** can nearly always replace **but**, but not vice versa. When **but** is used, it is nearly always after indefinite and interrogative pronouns/adverbs:

> **nobody but/except you would think of that**

> **what country but/except Italy has such magnificent architecture?**

> but only **except** is possible in, for instance:

> **you can all walk to the terminal except the old man here**

* **by**

> See also **at** and **from**.

i) **By** can be usefully compared with **on** in its use with words referring to means of transportation:

> **he goes by train**

> **is there only one conductor on this train?**

> **By** emphasizes the **means** of transport, and the noun following it normally has no article, except in a case like:

> **I'll be coming on/by the three-thirty**

> where the reference is not directly to the means of transport.

> Instead of **on**, **in** can be used if the idea of 'inside' is prominent:

> **it's often cold in British trains**

> Note also **live by** and **live on**. Live by means 'to **make** an income from', whereas **live on** means 'to **have** as one's only income or food'. Use of **by** emphasizes the means:

> **he lives by acting in commercials**

> **he lives by his pen**

he lives on £100 a month

he lives on fruit

Live by also means 'live according to the rules of':

it is difficult to live by such a set of doctrines

Compare **go by** in the sense of 'act according to':

you must go by the book

(once transformed into a neat pun to advertise a guide book:

GO BUY THE BOOK)

ii) passive:

By is used to indicate the agent or 'doer' (person or non-person) in passive constructions:

his reaction surprised us

we were surprised by his reaction

* **due to**

This is in competition with **owing to**:

this was due to/owing to his alertness of mind

Since **due** is an adjective, some people think it must behave like one (ie come in predicative position, after a form of the verb **be**), as in the example above, and is wrongly used in the example below. However, it is now increasingly common to use **due to** in adverbial structures in which it can be treated like a composite preposition such as **because of, in front of** etc:

the train was late, due to an accident near Bristol

* **during** see **for**
* **except** see **but**

★ **for**

i) When **for** refers to time, it can be usefully compared with **during** and **in**. **For** conveys the idea of period **length** (for how long?) whereas **during** means 'at one or several points in the course of' (when?):

for the first five months you'll be stationed at Crewe

during the first five months you're likely to be moved elsewhere

he let the cat out for the night

he let the cat out during the night

The emphasis on length of time that **for** conveys is also sometimes seen as a contrast to **in**, which means 'within (a period)':

I haven't seen her for five years

he didn't see her once in five years

compact discs will remain for the foreseeable future

recordable compact discs will appear in the foreseeable future

In American English, however, **in** would be normal in the first example:

I haven't seen her in five years

and this usage has also spread to British English.

For the use of **for/since** with expressions of past time see p 164.

ii) When **for** refers to place, it can be usefully compared with **to**:

(a) **the flight for/to Dublin is at 3 o'clock**

(b) **nothing went wrong on the flight to Dublin**

The difference is that **to** implies arrival at the destination, whereas **for** only expresses the plan or intention to go in the direction of that destination.

* **from**

  i) As we have seen before (see **by** above), **by** stresses the means and **from** indicates the source. Compare:

     judging by experience, this is unlikely to happen

     judging from earlier experiences, he had now learnt not to be so easily led astray

     Of course, sometimes there is little or no difference since the means/source distinction is not relevant:

     judging by his clothes, he must be poor

     judging from these figures, business is good

     The idea of source that **from** conveys is also seen when we contrast it with **of, by** and **with** in the following examples:

     the cat died from eating too much fish

     the cat died of cancer/by drowning

     the cat is trembling with fear

  ii) with **different**:

     Either **from** or **to** are used with **different**:

     that's different to/from mine

     that's different to/from what he said before

     But **than**, although commonly heard, is frowned upon by some.

* **in** and **into**

     For **in**, see also **at, by, for**.

     Basically **in** means 'confined within a certain place', whereas **into** implies moved from one certain place to another:

     he was sitting in the living room

     he went into the living room

No problem so far. However, in cases where the action implies movement from one place to another (and where we thus might expect **into**), we often use **in** if what is important is the **result** rather than the movement:

did you put sugar in my coffee?

Conversely, we sometimes use **into** when there is no verb of movement, but only if movement is implied. Compare:

you've been in the bathroom for an hour

the kitchen is awful, have you been into the bathroom yet?

Similarly, in the figurative sense:

he's into fast cars at the moment (= he's very interested in fast cars)

this will give you an insight into how the other half lives

★ **in front of** see **before**

★ **of** see **about** and **from**

★ **on** see **about**, **by** and **upon**

★ **opposite**

This is sometimes found with **to**, sometimes not:

the house opposite (to) ours is being pulled down

★ **outside**

This is frequently combined with **of** in American English, but not often in British English:

he reads a lot outside (of) his main subject area

★ **over** see **above** and **across**

★ **owing to** see **due to**

★ **since** see **after**

★ **till** see **to**

★ **to**

See also **for**, **from**.

When contrasted with **until/till**, **to** refers to a final point in time. **Until** and **till** also do this but there is typically a sharper focus on the activity expressed in the sentence:

he has one of those nine to five jobs

the shop is closed from 1 to 2 pm

he played his flute until 10 o'clock

last night I worked flat out from eight till midnight

There is no difference in meaning between **until** and **till**.

To in a different sense may have some similarity to **at** after certain verbs. In such cases **to** merely indicates direction towards a goal, whereas **at** is stronger in the sense that it denotes a desire, on the part of the 'doer', for stronger contact:

will we manage to get to her in time?

those boxes on top of the wardrobe – I can't get at them!

Note **get at** in two figurative senses:

why are you getting at me? (= why are you being so unkind to me in what you say?)

what are you getting at? (also **driving at** = what do you mean?)

★ **toward(s)**

See also **against**.

Toward is normally American English, **towards** British English.

★ **under** see **below**

★ **until** see **before** and **to**

★ **upon**

There is little difference in meaning between **upon** and **on** although **upon** is often a little more bookish or formal:

upon having, with great difficulty, reached Dover, he immediately set sail for France

what are your views upon . . .?

But **upon** also occurs in some (rather old-fashioned) set expressions (where **on** is not possible):

upon my word!

upon my soul!

Upon cannot replace **on** in the following meanings: (a) 'at the time of', (b) 'by means of' (see under **by** above), (c) implying a state, (d) 'with':

(a)   **can you come on Saturday?**

(b)   **he lives on fruit; our heaters run on gas**

(c)   **he's on the phone; it's on TV; he's on edge**

(d)   **have you got any money on you?**

If in doubt, **on** (with the exceptions above) is never wrong.

★   **with** see **from**

9. CONJUNCTIONS

Conjunctions join words, phrases or clauses. We distinguish between 'coordinating' conjunctions and 'subordinating'. Coordinating conjunctions join words and clauses that stand in equal relation to each other. Subordinating conjunctions join clauses that are dependent on other structures (normally other clauses). See further **Sentence Structure** p 241.

1 COORDINATING CONJUNCTIONS

These are either 'simple':

and, but, or, nor, neither

or 'correlative':

both . . . and, either . . . or, neither . . . nor

a) *Examples of simple coordinating conjunctions*

i) **you need butter and flour**
she's old and fragile
they followed fast and furious
they kept walking up and down the street
they ate and drank a great deal
they finished their work and then they went out to dinner

ii) **But** and **or** enter into the same combinations as **and**, eg:

she's plain but rich
trains going to or from London have been delayed

Note also the usage:

we can but try (= the least we could do is try)

iii) **Nor** is used before the second (or third etc) choice, after a **not** earlier in a sentence:

I don't eat sweets, nor chocolate, nor any kind of sugary thing

In this use **or** is also possible:

I don't eat sweets, or chocolate, or any kind of sugary thing

Nor is also used to join clauses, sometimes together with **and** or **but**. Note the inversion of subject and auxiliary verb:

I don't like coffee, nor do I like tea

I don't like coffee, (and) nor does she

I don't understand it, (but) nor do I need to

iv) **Neither** is used only as a clause connector:

I don't like coffee, neither does she

I don't understand it, (and/but) neither do I need to

v) If **(n)either ... (n)or** combine two nouns, the number of the verb follows the number of the noun nearer the verb:

either the record player or the loudspeakers have to be changed

either the loudspeakers or the record player has to be changed

b) *Examples of correlative coordinating conjunctions*

you need both butter and flour

she's both old and fragile

they both laughed and cried

you need either butter or margarine

she'll be either French or Italian

she was travelling either to or from Aberdeen

you need neither butter nor margarine

she's neither old nor fragile

it was done neither particularly well nor particularly badly

c) **Or** has four basic senses

i) The exclusive or alternative sense:

he lives in Liverpool or Manchester

ii) Similar to 'and':

you could afford things like socks or handkerchiefs or ties

iii) To combine synonyms:

rubella or German measles is a very infectious disease

iv) As a clause connector in the sense of 'if not' or 'otherwise':

apologize to her or she'll never speak to you again

2 SUBORDINATING CONJUNCTIONS

There are a great number of subordinating conjunctions. Some are 'simple', such as **because** or **so that**; others are correlative (compare 1 above), such as **as ... as**, **so ... that**, **more ... than**.

a) *Introducing noun clauses*

Noun clauses behave like (pro)nouns or noun phrases in a sentence. Compare:

(a) **I told him that they had done it**

(b) **I told him the facts**

In (a) a noun clause is the object of **told**, in (b) a noun (phrase).

The conjunctions that introduce noun clauses include **that**, **if**, **whether** and **how**. Of these **that** is sometimes omitted if its clause is the object of the sentence, but not if it is the subject:

he said (that) he wanted to see me (object)

that such people exist is unbelievable (subject)

he asked me if/whether I had any money (object)

whether I have any money or not is none of your business (subject)

he said how it was done (object)

how it's done is immaterial (subject)

That, **if**, **whether** and **how** as used above must not be confused with their roles in adverbial clauses (see below).

b) *Introducing adverbial clauses*

i) See **Adverbs and Adverbials**, p 71. There are a great number of conjunctions that introduce adverbial clauses, including many instances of nouns or verbs functioning as conjunctions, such as for instance **the minute** and **the way** in:

he arrived the minute the clock struck twelve (= conjunction of time, compare **when**) he didn't explain it the way you did (= conjunction of manner, compare **how**)

or **provided** and **considering** in:

provided you keep quiet, you can stay (= conjunction of condition, compare **if**)

he's doing well considering he's been here for only a week (= conjunction of concession, compare **although**)

The following are the most important adverbial-clause conjunctions:

ii) Conjunctions of time: **after, as, before, since, until, when, whenever, while**:

he came back after the show had finished
the phone rang as he was having a bath
before you sit down, you must see the bedroom
they've been crying (ever) since their parents left
he talked non-stop until it was time to go home
when he'd washed up, he sat down and lit his pipe
you don't have to go upstairs whenever the baby cries
while I'm asleep, will you drive?

iii) Conjunctions of place: **where, wherever**:

plant them where there is a lot of shade
wherever she goes, he follows

iv) Conjunctions of manner, comparison or degree: **as, as if, as though, how, however**:

he does it as he's always done it
he behaved as if/as though there was (were) something wrong
you can pay how you want
however hard you try, you won't manage

v) Conjunctions of reason: **as, because, only, since**:

as there was nothing but biscuits in the house, we went out to eat

I love you because you are you

I would have done it really, only I didn't think there was time

since you've been so kind to me, I want to give you a present

vi) Conjunctions of concession: **(al)though, even if, even though, whether**:

we let him stay (al)though he was a nuisance

you can stay, even if/even though you haven't paid your rent

I'm doing it whether you like it or not

vii) Conjunctions of purpose: **in order that, lest, so that**:

they went to the stage door in order that they could get a glimpse of him

I apologized lest she should be offended

he did it so that she would be happy

Note that **lest** tends to be rather literary usage. It is always possible to use **so that ... not** instead:

I apologized so that she shouldn't be offended

viii) Conjunctions of result: **so that**:

he somehow managed it so that they got together again

ix) Conjunctions of condition: **if, so/as long as, unless**:

only tell me if you want to

so/as long as you promise to be careful

tell me, unless you don't want to

c) **But** is a subordinating conjunction in the following senses

   i) 'without it being the case that' (after **never** and **hardly**):

   it never rains but it pours (proverb)
   hardly a day goes by but something happens

   ii) used with **that** (after certain negated nouns):

   there's no doubt but that he's responsible

d) *Introducing comparative clauses*

Subordinate comparative clauses do not modify other clauses (as adverbial clauses do); they modify clause elements: noun (phrases), adjective (phrases) and adverb (phrases).

The comparative conjunctions are correlative (compare **Coordinating Conjunctions**, 1 above, p 228): **more . . . than**, **less . . . than**, and **as . . . as**:

   i) Modifying a noun:

   they killed more people than we can imagine
   they killed as many people as the other side (did)

   ii) Modifying an adjective:

   it was less comfortable than we'd thought
   it was as comfortable as we thought

   iii) Modifying an adverb:

   you did it better than I could have done
   you did it as well as I could have done

10. NUMERALS

1 Cardinal and ordinal numbers

	cardinals	*ordinals*
1	one	first
2	two	second
3	three	third
4	four	fourth
5	five	fifth
6	six	sixth
7	seven	seventh
8	eight	eighth
9	nine	ninth
10	ten	tenth
11	eleven	eleventh
12	twelve	twelfth
13	thirteen	thirteenth
14	fourteen	fourteenth
15	fifteen	fifteenth
16	sixteen	sixteenth
17	seventeen	seventeenth
18	eighteen	eighteenth
19	nineteen	nineteenth
20	twenty	twentieth
21	twenty-one	twenty-first
30	thirty	thirtieth
40	forty	fortieth
50	fifty	fiftieth
60	sixty	sixtieth
70	seventy	seventieth
80	eighty	eightieth
90	ninety	ninetieth
100	a/one hundred	(one) hundredth
101	a/one hundred and one	(one) hundred and first
200	two hundred	two hundredth

1,000	a/one thousand	(one) thousandth
1,345	a/one thousand three hundred and forty-five	(one) thousand three hundred and forty-fifth

1,000,000	1,000,000,000 (9)	1,000,000,000,000 (10)
a/one million millionth	a/one billion billionth	a/one trillion trillionth

Note that **a billion** used to be (and sometimes still is) 10^{12} (ten to the power of twelve) and **a trillion** 10^{18} in British English. Those in the list are the American values, which are now being used in British English as well. 10^{9} used to be (and sometimes still is) called **a thousand millions** in British English.

2 Fractions

a) *Vulgar fractions*

Vulgar fractions are expressed by cardinal (sometimes **a** for **one**) + ordinal:

$\frac{1}{5}$ = **a/one fifth**

$\frac{3}{8}$ = **three eighths**

$3\frac{4}{9}$ = **three and four ninths**

$\frac{1}{2}$ = **a/one half**

$\frac{1}{4}$ normally = **a quarter**

$\frac{3}{4}$ = **three quarters**

Note 1 $\frac{1}{4}$ hours = **an/one hour and a quarter** or **one and a quarter hours**

Note the retention of **-s** when fractions are used as adjectives:

they had a two-thirds majority

b) *Decimals*

Whereas other European countries use a comma to represent the decimal point, English uses a full-stop:

25.5 = **twenty-five point five**

Digits after the decimal point are each said separately:

25.552 = twenty-five point five five two

3 Nought, zero, '0', nil

a) *British English*

Nought or **zero** is used for the actual figure or sign 0. In calculations **nought** is normal:

add another nought (or zero) to that number

put down nought and carry one

0.6 = nought point six

As a figure on a scale **zero** is preferred:

it's freezing − it's 10 below zero

as it is in scientific English:

given zero conductivity

an economy striving for zero inflation

When the figure is pronounced like the letter 'o', it normally refers to telephone numbers:

167205 = one six seven two 'o' five

Nil is always used to refer to points or goals in sport:

Arsenal won four nil (= 4-0)

or

Arsenal won by four goals to nil

except for tennis, which uses 'love':

Lendl leads forty-love

(This curious word is from French **l'oeuf** (the egg), a jocular reference to the shape of the figure.)

Nil is also used in the sense of 'nothing' (sometimes covered by **zero** also):

production was soon reduced to nil (or **zero**)

b) *American English*

Zero is used nearly everywhere:

> **how many zeros in a billion?**
>
> **my telephone number is 72102 (seven two one zero two)**
>
> **Chicago Cubs zero** (baseball score)

However, in tennis the word **love** is used, see p 237.

4 Dates

a) *Years*

1989 is spoken:

> **nineteen eighty-nine**

or, less commonly:

> **nineteen hundred and eighty-nine**

1026 is spoken:

> **ten twenty-six**

Here the use of **hundred** is not standard.

b) *Months and days*

There are several ways of writing dates:

12(th) May	**the twelfth of May**
May 12(th)	**May the twelfth**

In spoken American English it is commoner to omit the word 'the' when the month comes first:

> **May 12** (spoken: May twelfth/May twelve)

In British English dates are written numerically with the day first, in American English the month comes first:

> **10/4/89** (= 10th April 1989, British)
>
> **4/10/89** (= 10th April 1989, American)

5 Telephone numbers

Telephone numbers are spoken as single digits:

1567 = one five six seven

40032 = four double 'o' three two (British English)
four zero zero three two (American English)

But when they are written it is normal to break them up into groups of digits according to the various area codes in operation in a particular area:

041-221-5266

6 Calculations

There are several ways of expressing the basic arithmetical operations. Here are some of the commonest:

12 + 19 = 31
twelve and/plus nineteen is/equals thirty-one

19 − 7 = 12
nineteen minus seven is/equals twelve

seven from nineteen is/leaves twelve

nineteen take away seven is/leaves twelve (more colloquial)

2 x 5 = 10
twice five is ten

4 x 5 = 20
four times five is/equals twenty

four fives are twenty

36 x 41 = 1476
thirty-six times forty-one is/equals one thousand four hundred and seventy-six

thirty-six multiplied by forty-one is/equals one thousand four hundred and seventy-six

10 ÷ 2 = 5
ten divided by two is/equals five

two into ten goes five (more colloquial)

7   For **hundred**, **thousand**, **million** (**billion**, **trillion**) with or without **-s**, see **Nouns**, p 42. Compare further:

> **first they came in ones and twos, but soon in tens − at last in tens of thousands**
>
> **in the 1950s** (= nineteen fifties)
>
> **she's now in her eighties** (= between 80 and 90 years old)

8   **'The former' and 'the latter'**

Instead of **the first** we use **the former** when referring to one out of two persons or things just mentioned; and **the latter** (instead of **the last**) when referring to the second of two:

> **trains and coaches are both common means of transport − the former are faster, the latter less expensive**

Of the two expressions **the latter** is used more often, and can also refer to the last out of more than two:

> **Spain, Italy, Greece: of these countries the latter is still the most interesting as regards . . .**

Nouns may follow **the former/the latter**:

> **of the dog and the cat, the former animal makes a better pet in my opinion**

9   **'Once' and 'twice'**

Once is used for 'one time', **twice** for 'two times'. **Thrice** meaning 'three times' is archaic:

> **if I've told you once, I've told you a thousand times**
>
> **I've only seen her twice**

11. SENTENCE STRUCTURE

1 Clauses

Sentences consist of clauses. The essence of a clause is **subject** and **verb**, eg:

he smokes

We distinguish between main clauses and subordinate clauses, the latter being dependent on other structures. In:

he was crying because she had hit him

he was crying is the independent main clause (it could make up a perfectly good sentence on its own), and the remainder is a subordinate clause dependent on the main clause. There are three types (with various subtypes) of subordinate clause (shown in the examples outside the brackets):

i) noun clauses:

These fulfil the functions that nouns frequently have, such as subject, object and use after a preposition:

what he thinks (is of no importance to me) (subject)

(he said) **that he was ill** (object)

(are you surprised by) **what happened?** (after preposition)

ii) adjective clauses:

These are typically relative clauses (see further under **Relative Pronouns** p 115):

(that is the dog) **that did it**

But they may also be comparative clauses (see **Conjunctions**, p 234):

(we have less wine) than I thought

iii) adverbial clauses:

For more on these, see **Adverbs and Adverbials**, p 71, and **Conjunctions**, p 232:

(he switched on the light) so that they could read

(this is much more difficult) than I thought

2 Compound and complex sentences

A 'compound' sentence consists of two or more main clauses. The conjunctions used between them are coordinating conjunctions (see p 228):

he switched off the light and his wife put out the cat
(two main clauses)

Tom sulked, Dick complained, but Harry was happy
(three main clauses)

A 'complex' sentence consists of a main clause and at least one subordinate clause. A conjunction joining a main clause and a subordinate clause is a subordinating conjunction (see p 231):

Chris sulked   **when Alex told him off**
(main clause)   (subordinate clause)

3 Order of the clause elements/word order

a) *The subject*

i) The subject normally precedes both the auxiliary and the main verb:

he may smoke

Inversion of subject and verb takes place in the following cases (if there is one or more auxiliaries, inversion means that only the (first) auxiliary precedes the subject):

ii) in questions:

> **may I?**
>
> **(when) can you come?**
>
> **would you have liked to have had the chance?**

iii) in conditional clauses with **if** omitted:

> **had I got there in time, she'd still be alive**
>
> **should that be true, I'd be most surprised**

iv) when the sentence starts with a negative word or a word with negative meaning (such as **seldom**):

> **never did I think this would happen**
>
> **I can't swim − nor/neither can I**
>
> **little did I think this would happen**
>
> **hardly had he entered the room, when the ceiling caved in**
>
> **seldom have I enjoyed a meal so much**

But normal word order follows after **nevertheless**, **nonetheless** and **only**, all three of which refer to a previous statement:

> **I know he smokes, nevertheless/nonetheless he should be invited**
>
> **we'd like you to come, only we haven't got enough room**

v) often when the sentence starts with an adverbial of degree:

> **so marvellously did he play, that it brought tears to the eyes of even a hardened critic like me**
>
> **well, only too well, do I remember those words**

vi) sometimes, when the sentence starts with an adverbial, if the verb is without much descriptive meaning and the subject is relatively weighty:

> **in that year came the message of doom that was to change their world**

on the stage stood a little dwarf

out came a scream so horrible that it made my hair stand on end

to his brave efforts do we owe our happiness (rather literary)

to lend dramatic effect when there is an initial adverbial:

a big black car pulled up and out jumped Margot

vii) after initial **so** (= also):

I'm hungry — so am I

viii) in direct speech:

Sometimes after direct speech, the verb of utterance precedes its subject, especially if this is a noun (and the weightier the noun the more likely the inversion):

'you're late again', said John/John said

'you're late again!', boomed the furious sergeant (or the furious sergeant boomed)

But only normal word order is possible in the following sentence type:

'you're late again', John had said

If the subject is a pronoun, then the subject normally comes first:

'you're late again', he said

When the verb precedes a pronoun, it is frequently either because a relative clause follows or for jocular emphasis:

'you're late again', said I, who had been waiting for at least five hours

'I say *tomahtoes*', said she

'and I say *tomaytoes*', said he

Journalists are prone to cramming a lot of information into a subject (**vivacious blonde Mary Lakes from Scarborough said: '...'**). Since it is rather alien to English usage to place a word with so relatively little descriptive meaning as **said** so late in the sentence, journalists now often invert the order in such cases:

said vivacious blonde Mary Lakes from Scarborough:

If there is an adverbial, inversion is less common, but not unusual:

'you're back again', said John tentatively

But if there is an object, say after **ask** or **tell**, then inversion is not used:

'she is late again', John told the waiting guests

b) *The object*

The object normally follows the verb, but it receives initial position in the following cases:

i) in questions starting with an interrogative pronoun as object:

who(m) did you meet?

ii) in interrogative and relative subordinate clauses:

(please ask him) what he thinks

(can we decide) which position we're adopting?

(he brought back) what she'd given him

iii) for emphasis, especially when the object is **that**:

that I couldn't put up with

that I don't know

but his sort I don't like at all

iv) if the sentence contains both a direct and an indirect object, the indirect object precedes the direct if one (or both) is a noun:

he gave her a kiss

But if, instead of an indirect object, we have an adverbial prepositional phrase, this phrase comes last:

he gave the old tramp a fiver

or:

he gave a fiver to the old tramp

v) When the two objects are both pronouns, then the indirect precedes the direct:

could you please send her these in the mail tonight?

would you give me one?

well, tell them that then

he wouldn't sell me one

that secretary of yours, will you lend me her?

An exception to this is the use of 'it' with 'give' or 'lend' etc where there are two possibilities:

could you give it him when you see him?

could you give him it when you see him?

Of course it is also possible to say:

could you give it to him when you see him?

If 'to' is used then the word order is as in the example above.

he wouldn't sell one to me

c) *The adverbial*

For the position of adverbs, see p 92. When the adverbial is relatively heavy (often a prepositional phrase) then it does not normally split subject and verb:

he quickly left the room

he painfully realized what had happened

but:

in two quick leaps he was by her side

12. NOTES ON SPELLING

1   y to i

A **y** after a consonant changes to **i** before the following endings:

> -**able**, -**ed**, -**er** (both adjective and noun)
> -**est**, -**es** (both noun and verb)
> -**ly** and -**ness**

> **ply: plies: pliable**
> **cry: cried: cries: crier**
> **happy: happier: happiest: happily: happiness**

Exceptions:

shyly and **slyly** (**slily** is rare and best avoided). Conversely **drily** is more common than **dryly**:

Proper nouns ending in -**y** just add -**s**:

> **there were two Henrys at the party**

Compounds in -**by** add -**s**:

> **standbys, laybys**

Also **dyer** and sometimes **flyer** (also **flier**).

But **y** preceded by a vowel remains and the noun/verb ending is -**s** instead of -**es**:

> **play: plays: playable: player**
> **coy: coyer: coyest: coyly: coyness**

But note **lay: laid**, **pay: paid**, **say: said**, and **daily, gaily** (also **gayly**).

2 ie to y

This change takes place before -**ing**:

> **die: dying**, **lie: lying**

3 Dropping of final -e

Normally -**e** is dropped if a syllable starting with a vowel is added:

> **stone: stony**
>
> **love: loving: lovable**

But there are quite a few exceptions, such as **matey**, **likeable**, **mileage**, **dyeing** (= colouring — so as not to be confused with **dying**), **hoeing**, **swingeing** (so as not to be confused with **swinging**).

If the word ends in -**ce** or -**ge**, then the -**e** is retained before -**a** and -**o**:

> **irreplaceable**, **changeable**, **outrageous**

If the next syllable starts with a consonant, the -**e** normally remains:

> **love: lovely**
>
> **bore: boredom**

But again there are some important exceptions, especially:

> **due: duly**, **true: truly**
>
> **whole: wholly**, **argue: argument**

4 -our to -or

When an ending is added to some words in -**our**, the -**u** is dropped:

> **humour: humorist**
>
> **vigour: vigorous**

But there is an important exception to this in the word
colour:

> **colour: colourful: colourlessness: colourist**

There is no problem for the Americans, who have
dropped the **-u** altogether:

> **humor: humorist**

5   Doubling of consonants

After a short stressed vowel a final consonant is doubled
before **-er**, **-est**, **-ed**, **-ing**. Final **-r** is doubled after both
short and long stressed vowels:

> **fit: fitter: fittest: fitted: fitting**
>
> **begin: beginner: beginning**
>
> **occur: occurred: occurring**

but:

> **keep: keeper: keeping**

or:

> **cure: cured: curing**

because the vowels in those two words are long

and:

> **vomit: vomited: vomiting**

because the **-i** is not stressed.

In British English **-l** is doubled even in an unstressed
syllable:

> **revel: revelled: reveller: revelling**
>
> **travel: travelled: traveller: travelling**

This doubling of **-l** does not take place in American
English:

> **travel: traveled: traveler: traveling**

Note also:

> **kidnap: kidnapped: kidnapper** (British English)
> **kidnap: kidnaped: kidnaper** (American English)

6 c to ck

Words ending in **-c** change the **-c** to **-ck** before **-ed**, **-er**, **-ing**:

> **frolic: frolicked: frolicking**
> **picnic: picnicked: picnicker: picnicking**

7 American variants

In addition to the American variants in 4 and 5 above, the following should be mentioned:

a) British English **-gue**, American English **-g**:

> **catalogue: catalog**

b) British English **-tre**, American English **-ter**:

> **centre: center**

c) British English **-nce**, American English **-nse** in:

> **defence: defense**
> **offence: offense**
> **pretence: pretense**

d) A few individual words. The first in each pair is British English:

> **cheque: check**, **cigarette** (American also)**: cigaret**
> **pyjamas: pajamas**
> **practise** (ie the verb)**: practice** (the noun has **-ce** on both sides of the Atlantic)
> **programme: program** (but in computing also **program** in British English)
> **tyre: tire**

INDEX

a 17-21
-able 66
about 214-215
absolute 56
absolute superlative 64
abstract concepts 66
abstract nouns 29-30
accusative with
  infinitive 140-141
active 139
adjective clause 241-242
adjectives 56-70, 153,
  155
adjectives as nouns 66-
  70
adverbial clauses 71, 73-
  74, 232-234, 242
adverbial functions 77
adverbial phrases 71-73,
  246
adverbs 71-99, 144, 153
adverbs of degree 72,
  95-98
adverbs of manner 72,
  93-95
adverbs of place 72, 93
adverbs of time 72, 92
after 216, 220, 232
all 18, 126-128
although 232-233
always 162
American English 38,
  108, 140, 148, 169, 184,
  205, 223, 225, 226, 236,
  238-239, 249-250
among(st) 217
an 17-21
and 110, 143, 228-230
animal names 41-42
another 128-129
any 120-123
anybody, anyone 101,
  106, 120-121
anything 120, 122-124

anything + infinitive
  179-180
apposition 20
appositional adjectives
  65-66
articles 17-28
as 18, 110, 232-233
as . . . as 231, 234
as if/though 174, 233
aspect 138
attitudinal past tense 176
attributive adjectives
  58-62, 64-65
auxiliaries 135, 156-158,
  170, 204, 212-213
base 133-134, 136-137,
  144
be 135, 139, 151, 173,
  180-181, 212
be about to 169
because 231, 233
been 212
before 219, 232
be going to 167-169
believe 142, 159
be said to 142
beside 220
besides 220
be to 169
both 18, 130-131, 230
but 221, 228-229, 234
by 218, 221-222, 224
calculations 239-240
can 135, 189-191
can't 158, 189
cardinal numbers 235-
  236
causative 184
class 19-20
clause 241-242
collective nouns 38-39
comma 151-152
commands 186

common nouns 30
comparative 56, 128
comparative clauses 234
comparison 56-58, 62-
  64, 75-76
complex sentence 242
compounds 46-47
compound sentence 242
concrete nouns 29
condition 145, 151, 154,
  168, 170-173, 203
conjunctions 154, 228-
  234
continuity of action 164-
  167, 181
continuous verb forms
  151
contractions 99, 158,
  186, 189, 191, 195, 212-
  213
coordinating
  conjunctions 228-230,
  242
correlative coordinating
  conjunctions 230
could 135, 189-191
couldn't 189
countable nouns 30-38,
  67, 126
countries 26, 104
dare 137, 140, 196-197
dates 238
decimals 236-237
deduction 188, 194-195
defining clause 115-116
definite article 21-28
demonstrative
  pronouns 112-113
dice 44
did 213
different from/to 231
direct passive 177
dislike 149
distributive plural 48-49

do 135, 140, 156, 158-
161, 185, 196, 213
does 213
doesn't 213
done 213
don't 158-160, 213
double genitive 53, 111
doubling of consonants
249-250
due to 222
during 223
dynamic passive 177-
178
dynamic verbs 161-162
each 125-126
-ed 133, 136-137, 155
either 129-130
either . . . or 228-229
elder/eldest 63
elliptical clauses 144,
151, 154
emphatic 'do' 185
emphatic usage 109
enough 97-98
-er 56-57
-(e)s 40, 137, 139
-est 56-57
even if/though 233
-ever 115, 119
every 125, 126
everybody, everyone
126
everything 126-127
far 78
farther/farthest 62
fast 78
feminines 54-55
few 21, 32, 34
fewer 33-34
for 144, 216, 223
forever 162
former 240
fractions 236
French words 41
further/furthest 62
future continuous 166-
167
future perfect(ive)
(continuous) 169
future simple 166-167

future time 165-172
generic usage 19, 22,
105-108
genitive 50-54
gerund 136, 145-150,
153, 159
get 177-178, 184
gradable adjectives 62
gradable adverbs 71
Greek words 44-46
group genitive 54
had 172-173, 213
had better/best 140
hadn't 213
had rather +
subjunctive 174
half + article 19
hard(ly) 84, 234
have 135, 140, 154, 178,
181-184, 213
have got 182-183
have got to 193-194
haven't 213
have to 193-194, 204
he 100-101, 103-104
her(s) 111
his 111
hope 149, 159
how 198, 231, 233
however 233
I 100-102
-ible 66
I'd 213
if 154, 168,170-173, 231,
232-234
if + subjunctive 175-176
if need be 174
if only 174
imperative 103, 139,
158, 160, 171, 180
in 218, 221, 223-225
indefinite article 19-21
indefinite pronouns
120-132
indicative 138-139
indirect passive 177
indirect questions 157
indirect speech 193,
202-204
infinitive 136, 140-145,

147-150, 159, 179-180
infinitive continuous
138, 140
infinitive perfect(ive)
138-139
infinitive perfect(ive)
continuous 138
infinitive simple 138-139
-ing 136, 146, 153
in order that 233
in order to 143
interrogative pronouns
113-115, 156
into 224-225
intonation 96, 151, 156
inversion 185, 229, 242-
245
irregular comparison
58, 76
irregular verbs 133-134,
205-212
it 104-105
Italian words 45
its 111
it's time + subjunctive
175
keep 149
last 62
later/latest 62
Latin words 44-46
latter 62-63, 240
less 33-34
less/lesser 63
less . . . than 234
lest 233
let 140
let's 160
like (verb) 142
like (prep) 110
little 21, 32-33, 78
-ll 165-168
long 78
-ly 74
main verb 135
make 140
many 18, 33
may 135, 190, 191-193
me 100-101
measurement words 42
might 135, 191-193

mine 111
modal auxiliaries 135,140, 186-197, 202
months 238
mood 138-139
more 56-57
more . . . than 231, 234
most 56-57, 86-87
much 32-33, 96-97, 155
must 135, 140, 193-195, 204
my 111
nationalities 67-70
need 137, 140, 196-197
negations 158-161, 180, 182
negative comparison 58
neither 129-130, 228-229
neither . . . nor 228-230
never 160-161, 196, 234
nevertheless 243
nil 237
no 124
non-defining clause 115-116
none 124-125, 128
non-gradable adverbs 71
nor 229
not 98-99, 158-160, 195-196, 229
nothing + infinitive 180
nought 237
noun clauses 231, 241
nouns 29-55
nouns formed from adjectives 29
nouns formed from verbs 30
numerals 42, 235-240
object 245-246
obligation 188, 193-195
of 145, 215, 224
of-construction 51-52
omission of the article 23-28
omission of the relative 120
on 215, 221-222, 227

one 67, 129, 131-132
one (generic usage) 107-108
only 78, 96, 143, 233, 243
opposite 225
or 228-230
ordinal numbers 235-236
other(s) 128-129
ought to 135, 195
our 111
-our 248-249
ours 111
owing to 222
pair words 35
passive 139-140, 142, 154, 177-180, 184, 199, 222
past continuous 138-139, 163-164, 182
past participle 136, 154-155
past perfect(ive) 138, 165, 202-203
past perfect(ive) continuous 138-140, 145
past simple 138-139, 163-165
past tense 137, 173-176
past time 163-165, 172-173
pence 44
perfect(ive) 138, 154
personal pronouns 100-109
phrasal verbs 197-201
place names 26
pluperfect 138
plural 40-50
plurals in -a 44-45
plurals in -e 45
plurals in -en 44
plurals in -(e)s 40
plurals in -i 45
plurals in -im 46
plurals of compounds 46-47
plural verb 36-37
'point of view' verbs

142, 159, 161
possessive 146-147
possessive adjectives 111
possessive pronouns 111
possibility 170-172, 190-191, 192
postmodification 49-50, 145
predicative adjectives 58, 61-62, 64-65
prefer 142
premodification 49-50
prepositional phrase 22, 214
prepositional verbs 197-201
prepositions 150, 214-227
present continuous 138, 161-162, 168-169, 182
present participle 136, 141, 147, 151-153
present perfect(ive) 138-139, 164-165, 202
present perfect(ive) continuous 138, 140, 164
present simple 138-139, 161-162, 168
present tense 137
present time 161-163, 170-172
primary auxiliaries 135
probability 188, 194, 195
progressive 138
prohibition 194
pronouns 102-132
proper nouns 30
provided 232
putative use of 'should' 188-189
questions 156-158, 167, 180, 182, 187, 243
question-tags 157-158, 182-183
quick(ly) 76, 87
quite 18
rather 18
reflexive pronouns 100, 109-110

reflexive verbs 110
regular verbs 133
relative pronouns 115-120, 200
reported speech 202-204
requests 166-167, 171, 176, 187
-'s 50-54
seasons 24
seldom 243
sentence structure 241-246
sex of nouns 54-55
shall 135, 165-168, 170, 187-189, 202
shan't 187
she 103-104
should 135, 171-172, 175, 187-189, 204
shouldn't 187
since 216, 232-233
singular 48-50
slow(ly) 76, 90
so 18, 108
so as to 143
so long as 233
some 120-123, 129
somebody 120, 129
someone 129
something 122-124
something + infinitive 180
so . . . that 231
so that 231, 233
spelling 247-250
split infinitive 144
stative passive 177-178
stative verbs 161
stress 147
subject 241, 242-245
subjunctive 138-139, 173-176
subordinating conjunctions 231-234, 242
such + article 18
suggestions 166, 191
superlative 56-58, 143
telephone numbers 237, 239
tense 138

tense change 202-204
than 110, 128
that 112-113, 115-117, 120, 142, 231, 234, 245
the 17-18, 21-28
their 106, 111
theirs 111
there is + noun + infinitive 179-180
these 112
they 106-107
they'd 213
they're 212
they've 213
think 159
this 112-113
those 112
though 233
till 226
to (with infinitive) 136, 144, 150
to (preposition) 150, 223-226
too 18
toward(s) 217, 226
try 143, 148, 149
twice 240
uncountable nouns 30-38, 45, 126
unless 170, 233
until 219, 226, 232
upon 227
used to 163, 195-196
verbal nouns 145
verbs 133-213
very 96-97, 155
voice 139-140
vowel change 42, 133-134
vulgar fractions 236
want 142, 149
watch 141
we 105-106, 152
what 18, 114-115, 119, 198
whatever 115, 119
when 154, 168, 198, 232
whenever 232
where 198, 232
wherever 232

whether 231, 233
which 114-119
whichever 119
while 232
who 113, 115-117, 198
whoever 115, 119
whole 127
whom 113, 116
whose 114, 117-118
why (not) + infinitive 141
will (future) 165-169
will (conditional) 170-171
will (modal auxiliary) 135, 158, 186-187
-wise 76
wish 142, 149
wish + subjunctive 174
wishes 193
with 224
won't 158-159
word order 242-246
worth 150
would 135, 158, 163, 170-172, 186-187, 204
would best 140
wouldn't 186
years 238
you 105
your(s) 111-112
zero 237-238

HARRAP'S ENGLISH STUDY AIDS

In the same series:

ENGLISH VERBS
★ 1,000 phrasal verbs with definitions and examples
★ Verb formation
★ Tense usage
★ Index to verb patterns and forms

142mm × 96mm/256pp/plastic cover
ISBN 0 245-54745-2

BASIC ENGLISH VOCABULARY
★ 2,000 frequently used words
★ Thousands of other words formed from the main words
★ Many examples to show how each word is used
★ Short notes to explain language problems
★ Exercises and key

142mm × 96mm/331pp/plastic cover
ISBN 0 245-54747-9

MINI ENGLISH DICTIONARY
★ 125,000 words and meanings
★ Totally modern vocabulary
★ Definitions for every word
★ Phonetic transcriptions

142mm × 96mm/633pp/plastic cover
ISBN 0 245-54587-5

ENGLISH SPELLING
★ Nearly 30,000 alphabetical entries
★ Colour-coded to identify common spelling mistakes
★ Helpful hints for improving spelling
★ Words of similar sound and meaning simply explained

142mm × 96mm/abt 400pp/plastic cover
ISBN 0 245-54832-7

ENGLISH SYNONYMS
★ 8,000 key words alphabetically listed
★ Synonyms grouped according to meaning
★ Parts of speech specified for each key word
★ Clear distinction between literal and figurative meanings

142mm × 96mm/abt 400pp/plastic cover
ISBN 0 245-54831-9

ENGLISH USAGE
★ Over 4,000 alphabetical entries
★ Practical guidance on all aspects of usage
★ Clear examples to illustrate spelling and grammar rules
★ Coverage of foreign and scientific terms

142mm × 96mm/abt 400pp/plastic cover
ISBN 0 245-54830-0